THE LORD'S PRAYER

The Lord's Prayer

Perspectives for Reclaiming
Christian Prayer

Edited by

Daniel L. Migliore

William B. Eerdmans Publishing Company
Grand Rapids, Michigan

The contents of this volume first appeared as a special issue of
The Princeton Seminary Bulletin (Supplementary Issue No. 2, 1992)
and are reprinted by permission.

Library of Congress Cataloging-in-Publication Data

The Lord's Prayer: perspectives for reclaiming Christian prayer /
edited by Daniel L. Migliore.
p.   cm.
"The contents of this volume first appeared as a special issue of
The Princeton Seminary Bulletin (Supplementary Issue No. 2, 1992)" — p. iv.
Includes bibliographical references.
ISBN 0-8028-0119-6
1 Lord's Prayer — Criticism, interpretation, etc.   I. Migliore, Daniel L., 1935-
BV230.L56   1993

226.9'606 — dc20   93-26628
CIP

CONTENTS

Preface   1
   Daniel L. Migliore

The Lord's Prayer in Our Time: Praying and Drumming   5
   Jan Milič Lochman

Enthroned on the Praises and Laments of Israel   20
   Samuel E. Balentine

Jewish Prayers in the Time of Jesus   36
   James H. Charlesworth

The Lord's Prayer in the Gospels of Matthew and Luke   56
   Donald Juel

The Lord's Prayer in Patristic Literature   71
   Karlfried Froehlich

John Calvin's Teaching on the Lord's Prayer   88
   Elsie Anne McKee

Pastoral Theology and the Lord's Prayer   107
   Patricia Wilson-Kastner

The Theology and Ethics of the Lord's Prayer   125
   Douglas John Hall

Selected Bibliography   137
   Steven Richard Bechtler

Contributors   151

PREFACE

Prayer is essential to Christian life. When we pray, we lift our hearts to God as alone the source of our life and our salvation. So important is prayer that John Calvin speaks of it as the chief exercise of faith. Echoing this judgment, Karl Barth describes prayer as our response to the gracious God that must precede, accompany, and follow all else that we do. Just as Christians would lose their identity if they no longer attended to the proclamation of the gospel, the celebration of the sacraments, and the ministry of compassion to the needy, so the practice of calling upon God is for Christians as necessary as breathing in and out.

While prayer is a universal religious phenomenon, Christians of every age have felt the need for guidance in the practice of prayer. Like the first disciples, they have asked of Jesus, "Lord, teach us to pray" (Lk. 11:1), and they have found in the Lord's Prayer the help and the direction that they have sought. Many prominent theologians of the church, from Origen and Augustine, to Francis and Thomas, to Luther and Calvin, to Barth and Boff, have written commentaries on the Lord's Prayer and praised its excellence as a guide to the Christian practice of prayer. For Tertullian the Lord's Prayer offered a breviary of the whole gospel; Luther said that he never ceased to feed on this prayer as a child sucks nourishment from its mother; Calvin wrote of the Lord's Prayer that it far surpassed all others in perfection; and Barth, who praised the Lord's Prayer as the "incomparable text" of prayer, was engaged in an extensive commentary on this text when poor health forced him to discontinue his writing of the *Church Dogmatics*.

As is true of all the texts of faith, the Lord's Prayer invites and requires fresh interpretation in every age. The church of our time brings its own special experiences and struggles to this interpretive task. Several marks of the Lord's Prayer seem especially relevant to our spiritual situation at the close of the twentieth century.

For one, the Lord's Prayer is emphatically a *we* prayer, a prayer that we utter as members of the people of God rather than as isolated individuals. We pray as a community and on behalf of all humanity and, indeed, of all creatures. Not a trace of individualism is evident in this prayer. There is no search for personal salvation apart from the renewal of the life of the whole creation. The Lord's Prayer is thus a prayer not of individualistic piety but of solidarity in suffering and hope with the entire groaning creation.

The Lord's Prayer is also unmistakably a *theocentric* prayer. We recognize today how strong the current of anthropocentrism has been in much traditional Christian theology and spirituality. In the prayer that Jesus taught his disciples, however, humanity and its well-being are not elevated above all else. On the contrary, prayer for the hallowing of God's name, for the coming of God's reign, and for the doing of God's will takes precedence over the petitions for the well-being of humanity. By calling us to attend first to God's honor and reign, and by summoning us to see ourselves — our needs and our desires — in relation to God's purposes for the whole creation, the Lord's Prayer continually reforms our spirituality and our theology.

A closely related mark of the Lord's Prayer is its holistic understanding of human salvation. Just as this prayer sets the well-being and fulfillment of humanity within the encompassing horizon of God's purposes for the whole creation, so it expands our understanding of salvation beyond every kind of dualism. It encourages us to think holistically rather than dualistically about the purposes of God and human salvation. Our flourishing as human beings includes both physical and spiritual well-being. Petitions for daily bread (i.e., whatever is necessary for our physical well-being) and forgiveness of sins (i.e., the acceptance and empowerment that we need from God and from each other to begin life anew again and again) are not to be played off against each other. We pray for wholeness of body and spirit and for renewal of both personal and public life because these are equally important and mutually dependent dimensions of salvation.

When spoken from the depths of our own need and in solidarity with the poor of the earth whose voices have long been silent, the Lord's Prayer proves to be a profoundly liberating prayer. Called to prayer, we are summoned not to passivity but to activity, not to bondage but to freedom, not to indifference about evil in and around us but to passion for justice, freedom, and peace in the whole creation. Prayer modeled after the Lord's Prayer is the ever-new beginning of our participation in the work of God in the world. It is the beginning of active partnership with God who wills to be God with us, not apart from us.

In the essays collected in this volume, eight prominent theologians explore these and other aspects of the Lord's Prayer. They underscore its communal character, its rich Old Testament background in the lament and praise of Israel, its immediate context in the piety and prayer life of Judaism of the first century, its hermeneutical key in the gospel narrative of Jesus' ministry, death, and resurrection, its remarkable vitality in shaping the prayer and practice of Christians for two millennia, its integration of realism and hope, and its coupling of the glory of God and the renewal of humanity and all creation. Careful study and meditation on the Lord's Prayer such as provided by the contributers to this volume should help us to reclaim Christian prayer for our time not as an escape from responsibility but as an exercise of Christian freedom and as the beginning of all true knowledge and glad service of God.

Presented at the 1991 Frederick Neumann Symposium on the Theological Interpretation of Scripture held in Princeton, these essays were previously published in the *Princeton Seminary Bulletin,* Supplementary Issue, No. 2 (1992). Their reprinting is a response to many requests to make this material available to a wider public.

DANIEL L. MIGLIORE
Arthur M. Adams Professor of
Systematic Theology
Princeton Theological Seminary

The Lord's Prayer in Our Time: Praying and Drumming

by JAN MILIČ LOCHMAN

I. THE AMBIGUITY OF PRAYER

IN OUR time, theology of prayer (and even prayer itself) seems to face an ambiguous situation. Prayer is undoubtedly one of the oldest and most constant phenomena in the history of religion and culture. It is no wonder that the church father Tertullian, contemplating the varied but impressively universal presence of attitudes of prayer in all nations, made his famous remark about the witness of the *"anima naturaliter christiana"* (the soul that is by nature Christian). In our century, Friedrich Heiler, the classical representative of a theology of prayer, ventured in 1965 a similar categorical statement: "The human instinct of prayer is ineradicable. ... Prayer is meaningful and necessary also for modern people."[1] He seems to be right. Even in our secularized age prayer has not completely disappeared or become completely homeless. In recent years, even the unchurched have shown increased interest in spiritual exercises and meditation.[2]

However, there is another side to this situation. Understood in the precise sense, as direct and purposeful invocation of God, prayer has become less intelligible and even less believable to many people today. This applies even to some developments in our contemporary theology. The monographic article on prayer in the current *Theologische Realenzyklopädie* has to acknowledge: "Hardly any modern Protestant dogmatics contains a special chapter on prayer in which fundamental questions of a theology of prayer would be dealt with."[3] Even theologians who try to overcome such a negligence, like

---

[1] F. Heiler, "Das Gebet in der Problematik des modernen Menschen," in *Interpretation der Welt: Festschrift für Romano Guardini zum achtzigsten Geburtstag*, ed. H. Kuhn, H. Kahlefeld, and K. Forster (Würzburg: Echter-Verlag, 1965), pp. 231, 243.

[2] Another version of unexpected interest in prayer in a secularized society emerged in the course of the Christian-Marxist dialogue in the sixties. Milan Machovec, a Marxist partner in this dialogue, emphasized the paramount significance of prayer for human self-understanding. However, he did so from a strictly atheistic point of view. For him "prayer" was not a dialogue between two distinct partners, the human person and God. It was rather an "inward demystified dialogue" between the empirical and ideal self. In this sense he was able to state: "Without prayer, we are poorer"; but it is clear that by "prayer" he somehow ambiguously understood acts of subjective meditation. See M. Machovec, "Gebetsanleitung für Atheisten," *Neues Forum* 14 (1967): 574ff.

[3] G. Müller, "Gebet VIII: Dogmatische Probleme gegenwärtiger Gebetstheologie," in

Gerhard Ebeling, speak of the "widest spread of prayerlessness"[4] or, as
C. H. Ratschow, of the danger that "in our times prayer seems to die out."[5]

There are many cultural and spiritual reasons for such ambiguous developments. Dorothee Sölle has drawn attention to one of the most important
in her essay "Gebet."[6] For the modern post-Christian consciousness, she
writes, prayer has become a substitute action. Where the captain of a ship
in distress says that the only thing to do is to pray, the cry goes up from the
chaplain: "Are things that bad?" This anecdote describes the situation
rather accurately. God is brought in when human intelligence and power
cannot do anything, or can no longer do anything. Prayer comes into action
when our own strength fails. In place of responsible secular action prayer
has a role in certain emergency situations, but only as an illusion, a flight, a
substitute action when we are not capable of real action or not willing to
engage in it.

A familiar incident in Brecht's *Mother Courage* illustrates how little credibility prayer has when it is viewed in this way. A group of helpless peasants
faces advancing soldiers. It seems that nothing could be done to prevent the
shedding of blood. The peasants are weak and have no weapons; they have
nothing on which to rely. They give up and pray. Even the dumb Kattrin
is urged to pray. But instead of praying, she begins to beat on a drum in
order to awaken the inhabitants. She is shot down, but the city is ready to
resist.

Dorothee Sölle comments that this extreme case brings to light an old
misunderstanding of prayer, namely, that of substituting words to a higher
being for acts on behalf of those around us. The drumming of Kattrin shows
that devout and subjectively genuine prayer must not be an excuse for those
who do not want to become involved. If we ask Christians what they did
for Jews during the persecution, the most mendacious answer is: "We
prayed for them."[7]

In these deliberations Sölle is close to Dietrich Bonhoeffer. In his *Letters
and Papers from Prison* Bonhoeffer writes very impressively about the way
in which religious themes like God and prayer have been pushed into a
corner in the course of contemporary secularization. They are little more

---

Theologische Realenzyklopädie (Berlin and New York: Walter de Gruyter, 1984), vol. 12, p.
85.

[4] G. Ebeling, *Dogmatik des christlichen Glaubens* (Tübingen: J. C. B. Mohr [Paul Siebeck],
1979), vol. 1, p. 196.

[5] C. H. Ratschow, *Leben in Glauben* (Stuttgart and Frankfurt, 1978), p. 143.

[6] D. Sölle, "Gebet," in *Theologie für Nichttheologen* (Stuttgart, 1966), pp. 102ff.

[7] Sölle, "Gebet," p. 103.

than stopgaps (and prayer is a substitute action). To most thinking people they are beyond belief. A world come of age needs a religionless interpretation of the Christian cause. For Bonhoeffer this is the real challenge to modern theology. But for him (and for Sölle) this task does not mean giving up prayer. It means a more relevant and credible readoption of it, not in an unenlightened, generally religious, magical, or self-centered sense, but in the sense of the Bible and Jesus, as an act of the heart that is moved on behalf of justice. Bonhoeffer finds the basic structure of the Christian life in the prayer and action of the righteous. As he pithily puts it, "Only he who cries out for the Jews may sing Gregorian chants."[8]

But those who *do* cry out for the Jews, those for whom doing righteousness in a social context is important, *may and should* sing Gregorian chants. If prayer is highly suspect as a substitute for responsible action, then an activism without the perspective of prayer—an evasive busyness as a substitute for prayer—is also a theological temptation, and one that perhaps today is no less real than the first. The example of Bonhoeffer himself helps us to avoid drawing too hasty a conclusion. The papers from prison include many poems and prayers that clearly focus on this concern of Christian existence. The witness of those around him bears out this impression. I will cite only that of the prison doctor in the last minutes before Bonhoeffer's execution.

> Through the half-open door in one room in the huts I saw Pastor Bonhoeffer, before taking off his prison garb, kneeling on the floor praying fervently to his God. I was deeply moved by the way this lovable man prayed, so devout and so certain that God heard his prayer. ... In the almost fifty years that I worked as a doctor, I have hardly ever seen a man die so entirely submissive to the will of God.[9]

This example might help to elucidate the place of prayer in our post-Christian culture, or, better, our own situation as we engage in prayer today. There can be no doubt, says Sölle, that with a better understanding of the world the things in uncontrolled nature that drove us to prayer are far fewer. Quantitatively there are probably fewer individuals praying now than for hundreds of years. But this less can be more. For as the scope for the remaining magical elements and incantations has shrunk, a more enlightened reflection might help prayer to come to its true self.[10]

[8] E. Bethge, *Dietrich Bonhoeffer: Man of Vision, Man of Courage* (New York: Harper & Row, 1970), p. 512.
[9] Bethge, *Dietrich Bonhoeffer*, pp. 830-831.
[10] Sölle, "Gebet," p. 103.

II. The Modes of Prayer

"Help prayer to come to its true self." But what is prayer according to the Bible? Let us attempt a short sketch.

Prayer is the response and vital side of faith. Believers pray; those who pray believe. "I believe, Lord; help thou mine unbelief" (Mk. 9:24). This classical New Testament confession of faith is a prayer. It shows the place of prayer. Its context is our need or necessity before God. If we do not feel and recognize this need, prayer ceases or is perverted. It *ceases* if we think we can lay aside the question of God as an outdated and meaningless question of our own cultural history or the history of world culture. It is *perverted* when the devout or orthodox (the self-righteous) believe they can meet their need before God by merits or credits. When we think that our own verdict can bind God and his judgment, the praise of God becomes self-praise, pseudo-prayer. We recall the story of the Pharisee and the publican (Lk. 18:9-14). When we either cease to pray or pervert prayer, the unrest of faith is stabilized, the tension of the question of God is released. Self-confirmation is found in either our "having" or our "not having."

Prayer is a protest against such self-confirmation. It is a step into the open, with no guarantee but also without resignation. It is part of the battle for God, like Jacob's wrestling at the Jabbok and saying "I will not let you go, unless you bless me" (Gen. 32:26). Those who wrestle and pray biblically do not rely on their own virtues or the ardor of their practice of piety but on the promise that is given them. Luther expressed this when he said that he dared to pray to God, not because of his own devotion or holiness, but because from the lips of God's Son had come the promise that those who ask, receive. The heart might not be ardent or fervent enough, but Luther built upon the Word.[11]

In this sense biblical prayer is more than verbal prayer. The apostle speaks about praying without ceasing (1 Thess. 5:17). Clearly we have here a whole dimension of human existence before God. Prayer as this inner dimension embraces and accompanies the whole polyphony of human life. In this sense all thoughts and actions that respect God and his creation are acts of prayer. Prayer concerns what the Czech philosopher and statesman T. G. Masaryk continually described and lived out as life *sub specie aeternitatis*. Yet this understanding of our situation before God calls for concrete and specific

---

[11] M. Luther, "Predigt am Sonntag Vocem Iocunditatis," in *D. Martin Luthers Werke: Kritische Gesamtausgabe* (Weimar: Hermann Böhlaus Nachfolger, 1908), vol. 34, pt. 1, pp. 379-391.

expression, for prayer in the full sense of the word, for the articulated word of prayer. John Calvin bore impressive witness to this saving necessity of prayer, not as a duty, but as the liberating representation of God's all-embracing turning to us:

> Surely, with good reason the Heavenly Father affirms that the only stronghold of safety is in calling upon his name. By so doing we invoke the presence both of his providence, through which he watches over us and guards our affairs, and of his power, through which he sustains us, weak as we are and well-nigh overcome, and of his goodness, through which he receives us, miserably burdened with sins, unto grace.[12]

From this comprehensive and many-faceted nature of prayer, the various forms result. Of the biblical fulness, following 1 Tim. 2:1, we might mention especially three: petition, intercession, and thanksgiving.

It is to the human situation of need before God (and in God's world) that *petition* especially and directly relates. In the New Testament the range of petitionary prayer is very broad; it deals with small things and great. The apostle could pray that his plans for a journey might work out (Rom. 1:10), but we also find the prayer that the terrors of the last day will not come in winter (Mk. 13:18). There is confidence that the Father will see to our earthly welfare (Mt. 6:25-34), but prayer also for the coming of Christ (1 Cor. 16:22; Rev. 22:20).[13] Life in all its diversity is brought before God in petition.

No sphere of human life, and especially no urgent human need, lies outside prayer's terms of reference. Even fear of a magical misunderstanding of prayer ought not to cause us to make the spiritualizing or existentializing mistake of thinking it intellectually unworthy or theologically unenlightened to pray for specific physical and secular needs. The apostle is rightly much less inhibited when he tells us that if any are sick, then let them pray (Jas. 5:13-15). We see at once that any physical or mental illnesses are in view. The word of faith and promise applies to the sphere or material life as well: "The prayer of a righteous man has great power in its effects" (Jas. 5:16).

Along with petition stands *intercession*. The link between them is decisive

---

[12] J. Calvin, *Institutes of the Christian Religion*, ed. J. T. McNeill, trans. F. L. Battles, Library of Christian Classics, vol. 21 (Philadelphia: Westminster Press, 1960), vol. 2, p. 851 (III.20.2).

[13] Cf. E. Lohse, "Gebet III: Im NT," in *Evangelisches Kirchenlexikon*, ed. H. Brunotte and O. Weber, 2d ed. (Göttingen: Vandenhoeck & Ruprecht, 1961), vol. 1, p. 1436.

for our understanding of New Testament prayer. In prayer human need is not isolated; the personal and the social go together. People pray for one another in the Christian community, but they also pray for the world. Intercession is a sign of concerned participation in the fate of others. Jesus constantly laid this task upon the hearts of the disciples, and the apostles laid it upon the hearts of the churches. Prayer breaks through the narrow private area and becomes part of our social and political service of God: "First of all, then, I urge that supplications, prayers, intercessions, and thanksgivings be made for all men, for kings and all who are in high positions, that we may lead a quiet and peaceable life, godly and respectful in every way" (1 Tim. 2:1-2).

A further development along this line is the third form of prayer, *thanksgiving* and *praise*. Very concretely we have prayer here too. Faith is receiving and enjoying life with all its great and little opportunities as a gift that is ever new. Thanksgiving stands opposed to the way in which we, satiated and bored, take the everyday for granted, so that life becomes dull. But thanksgiving goes beyond that. Paul emphatically and constantly gives thanks for brothers and sisters in the faith, for the churches, even though they might disappoint him in many ways. Above all and in spite of everything he found a final and unconditional cause for thanksgiving in faith and in experience of the liberating nearness of God, of salvation in Christ, of hope for himself and the world. Logically, then, as we see especially in the Psalms and in New Testament doxologies, the final thing in prayer is praise of God.

In these three forms we have an outline of the basic structure of prayer from a biblical and theological standpoint. Petition, intercession, and praise: The plurality safeguards us against any impoverishment of the life of prayer. There are also other modes—for example, complaint. It, too, is prayer. The Bible neither forbids it nor censures it. Indeed, a whole biblical book bears the title Lamentations. There are also explicit songs of complaint and accusation in the Psalms. On the margin, and very problematical from the New Testament standpoint, though humanly understandable in the last resort, there are even psalms of revenge. Overcoming this human temptation has a place before God. Finally, not on the margin but at the center of the Bible, at the cross of Jesus Christ, there is the cry of dereliction: "My God, my God, why [to what end] hast thou forsaken me?" (Mk. 15:34; cf. Ps. 22:1). Unquestionably this cry from the depths, this protest against failure, betrayal, abandonment, and suffering, is also part of the fulness and totality of human life before God.

In this regard one should note that Christian prayer is more than an instrument and expression of the pious (or, in secular terms, the meditative) self-understanding. It does relate to the self, to the inner life of faith: "It's me, O Lord, standing in the need of prayer." But it is also a matter of our understanding of God and the world, of the need of others, of the glory of God. We should not play off these elements against one another or reduce them to one another. To use Anselmian language, prayer is not a *monologion* but a *proslogion*. In the quiet room we are not shut in with ourselves when we pray. On the contrary, we are alongside others and in the presence of God. This is the truly liberating aspect of prayer. Prayer is a special opportunity—made special by the promise—not to lose ourselves in our own wandering thoughts and self-seeking desires and expectations, but to be free of them.[14]

Understood in this way, prayer is a center of renewal for the life of faith in its biblical fulness. Without it faith would be no less dead than it would be without works. It gives us space. Our need for prayer is our need for spiritual and mental breath. In it we reach beyond ourselves to the promise of the Spirit that liberates *personally, socially*, and *theologically*.

In correspondence to the three main modes of prayer (petition, intercession, doxology) let us concentrate on these three dimensions of its liberating relevance.

III. Personal Identity and Prayer

In prayer we reach beyond ourselves, not to lose ourselves but to find ourselves. A vital question arises here, that of *our true identity* as human beings and as Christians. It is an urgent question today. Who am I? In the net of conditions and relations, of manipulations and determinations, who am I truly? Here again I find Dietrich Bonhoeffer especially helpful. In his *Letters and Papers from Prison* we find among his many prayers and verses the poem "Who am I?" In it he looks at the rift between the outward image that he presents and the way in which he understands and experiences himself. He cannot reconcile the two. A crisis of identity? The last lines of the poem read:

> Who am I? This or the other?
> Am I one person today, and tomorrow another?
> Am I both at once? A hypocrite before others,
> and before myself a contemptibly woebegone weakling?

[14] Cf. H. G. Ulrich, *Glaube und Lernen* 1 (1968): 17.

Or is something within me still like a beaten army,
Fleeing in disorder from victory already achieved?
Who am I? They mock me, these lonely questions of mine.
Whoever I am, thou knowest, O God, I am thine.[15]

The psalmists saw their lives like this. In the alternation of experiences, in the struggle for meaning and the orientation of existence, in contrasting situations and the clash of perspectives, they were who they were before God. In the light of the story of Christ, the apostle formulates precisely the same truth: "Your life is hid with Christ in God. When Christ who is our life appears, then you also will appear with him in glory" (Col. 3:3-4). Because this is so, because the identity of our life is grounded in God and thus persists through every temptation, attack, and break, prayer is an appropriate element and instrument of life for those in search of meaning.

In this insight and conviction Christians can follow the example and cling to the promise of Jesus. It is striking how important prayer was for Jesus, though he did not make a show of it. On the contrary, he sharply and emphatically attacked those who make prayer a spectacle—only hypocrites do that (Mt. 6:5-6). Yet he laid all the more emphasis on prayer as quiet, intense communion with God. The Gospels tell us again and again that Jesus withdrew to pray (e.g., Mk. 1:35 par.; Lk. 5:16), and even that he spent the whole night in prayer (Lk. 6:12). In critical hours especially he found in prayer new strength to withstand the assault of the tempter (Mt. 4:10 par.) or in severest temptation to win through to the will of the Father (Mk. 14:36 par.). Even his last words from the cross, whether the cry of dereliction in Mark, or "Father, into thy hands I commit my spirit" in Luke (23:46)—both quotations from the Psalms—are prayer.

Christians in prayer should have before them the promise as well as the precedent of Jesus. I have in mind the parting high priestly prayer in John 17, in which Jesus prays to the Father for his disciples, not merely for those present but also "for those who believe in me through their word" (v. 20). We may specifically think of the incident in Lk. 22:31-32. For the self-confident Simon who will soon deny Jesus, the hour of satanic sifting and bitter failure has the promise of a new beginning, not in Peter's own power but in the faithfulness of his Master: "I have prayed for you that your faith may not fail." According to the New Testament this is the basis and hope of the

[15] D. Bonhoeffer, *Letters and Papers from Prison*, ed. E. Bethge, enlarged ed. (London: SCM Press, 1971), p. 348.

Christian life. In spite of all our weaknesses we live and pray in the power of the prayer of Jesus.

It is in this light, in relation to Jesus, that we are to understand the direction and encouragement which transcend subjective helplessness and defeat and show us the right way in the search for personal identity: "Ask, and it will be given you; seek, and you will find; knock, and it will be opened to you. For every one who asks receives, and he who seeks finds, and to him who knocks it will be opened" (Mt. 7:7-8).

This appeal to God as the transcendent source and goal of human identity can gain a fresh relevance in our secularized culture. It helps us to see and to keep the boundary between legitimate secularity and totalitarian secularism in our political and individual lifestyles. In his dynamic exposition of the Lord's Prayer, Leonardo Boff makes this point convincingly. The prayer makes clear: "The last destiny of human beings is God. . . . In such understanding, we leave all totalitarianism of history behind us"—particularly the Marxian totalitarianism. "Human beings cannot be reduced to facts of history. . . . Human beings gain their truly essential humanity only in growing beyond themselves into the dimensions of God."[16] Prayer helps to keep open the full and free horizon of humanity.

IV. Social Implications of Prayer

The biblical vision of prayer has its unmistakable *social implications*. As in many other respects, "The Prayer of Prayers," the Lord's Prayer, is exemplary. It opens with an emphatic "our" and continues to the end not in the singular but in the plural. With this little word "our," Jesus resists any attempt to make the Prayer a purely private matter. The temptation is a considerable one both outwardly and inwardly. Do not people in both East and West argue that religion is a private concern? No one can forbid us to pray, but it is our own business. And are we not inwardly inclined to argue along the same lines: My prayer (or its absence) is no one else's business? The little word "our" challenges this privatizing attitude.

In his exposition of the Lord's Prayer, Leonhard Ragaz stressed especially the importance of this "our." The prayer, he said,

is not an egotistic religious prayer but a social Kingdom prayer. It is not an I prayer but a We prayer. It is not a prayer for me but a prayer for us. If we come before God in true prayer, we do not simply come before God who is our private God but before God who is the God of

[16] L. Boff, *Vater Unser: Das Gebet umfassender Befreiung* (Düsseldorf, 1981), pp. 80-81.

us all. He is the God who gathers us together with all his children, with our brothers and sisters. Thus the Lord's Prayer is the profoundest basis of true socialism.[17]

We are to think of the motif of the children of God in this regard. It is undoubtedly echoed in the invocation of the Lord's Prayer as a correlate of the name "Father." This expression might perhaps be misunderstood as implying elements of infantilism or immaturity. But the New Testament use points in a very different direction. The clearest apostolic references relate to the promise of freedom and maturity. I have in mind Galatians 4, where God's liberating movement in the sending of his Son aims at the mature freedom of the children of God: "And because you are children, God has sent the Spirit of his Son into our hearts, crying 'Abba! Father!' So you are no longer a slave but a child and if a child then also an heir through God" (4:67). There is no doubt that being a child is here the opposite of being a slave or being immature. Similarly, in Romans 8, that great chapter of hope, the cry "Abba, Father!" is seen as empowerment for freedom in the Spirit in the midst of the bondage of corruption to which, to the sighing of all creation, everything created is subject.

None of this is a self-evident matter of course. It is not a "broad road." It involves the narrow way of exodus and deliverance in virtue of being adopted sons and daughters that is granted in Jesus of Nazareth, also and above all in his cross and resurrection. Being a child of God is not, then, a common, ontologically given quality or *habitus* of the human race. It has a concrete basis in the incarnate Son and calls for a concrete response. This is made clear in the Johannine Prologue: "He came to his own home, but his own people received him not. But to all who received him . . . he gave power to become children of God" (1:11-12). This makes the "we" of the Lord's Prayer more precise. The emphatic subject of the Prayer is not a vague or cosmopolitan collective but the concrete fellowship of Christian brothers and sisters. The fact that in the early church the Lord's Prayer was not an "open prayer," but the prayer of the baptized at the eucharist, underlines this understanding.

Is it then a sectarian matter? The separation of a holy group from an unholy world? Not at all. The unmistakably concrete basis of being a child of God in the person and history of Jesus of Nazareth breaks down from the outset all the barriers that devout and sometimes self-righteous sectarians might want to erect around themselves. The path of Jesus was an initia-

[17] L. Ragaz, *Das Vaterunser*, Die Revolution der Bibel (Zürich, 1943).

tive of loving solidarity aimed not only at the near but also at the distant, including those written off by conventional morality and religion. The exclusiveness of God's fatherhood in Christ, and of the sonship and daughterhood based upon it, develops an inclusive dynamic which seeks conformity in the mind and acts of Christians (cf. Phil. 2:1-5). "Christians who regard themselves as ... good children of God [but] who refuse to sit with their Master at the table of publicans and sinners, are *not* Christians at all, have still to become so, and need not be surprised if heaven is gray above them and their calling upon God sounds hollow and finds no hearing."[18] The fatherhood of God that is open to us in Christ engenders a correspondingly open Christian family that strides across all frontiers. The little word "our," the "we" of the Lord's Prayer, is exclusively based but in this very fact it is an uncommonly inclusive word.

It is in this way that the social dimensions of prayer should be made relevant in Christian discipleship. I will sum it up in the remarkable words of Calvin:

Let the Christian people, then, conform their prayers to this rule in order that they may be in common and embrace all who are their brothers and sisters in Christ, not only those whom they at present see and recognize as such but all people who dwell on earth. For what God has determined concerning them is beyond our knowing except that it is no less godly than humane to wish and hope the best for them.[19]

V. Theology as Doxology

According to Gotthold Müller,

Praise of God (doxology) according to the witnesses of both Old (Ex. 15:18; Ps. 5:12; 93:1f; 96:10; 145:1 etc.) and New Testament (Matt. 6:13; Rom. 1:25; 11:36; 16:27; Gal. 1:15; 1 Tim. 1:17; Jud. 25; Rev. 7:12 etc.) is the only form of prayer enduring "from ages to ages." As faith and hope, all other forms of prayer (petition, intercession) come to their eschatological fulfillment and so to the end. What ultimately endures is the *doxa* of God which is, at the same time, the only true salvation of

[18] K. Barth, *Church Dogmatics*, vol. IV/4, *The Christian Life* (Grand Rapids: Wm. B. Eerdmans Publishing Co., 1981), p. 80.
[19] Calvin, *Institutes*, vol. 2, p. 201 (III.20.38).

humankind and of the whole creation: only in the *glorificatio Dei* occurs *salus hominum et mundi*.[20]

The Reformers, particularly those of the Reformed tradition, highlighted
the importance of the glorification of God as the ultimate goal of human
life. "Man's chief end is to glorify God, and to enjoy him forever" (Westminster Catechism). The summons *soli Deo gloria* and the vision of the
world as *theatrum gloriae Dei* were basic accents of classical Reformed piety.
The program of "glorification" was never restricted to one particular dimension, e.g., that of personal piety. It referred to human life in its wholeness, including its missionary, political, and "aesthetic" dimensions.[21]

In the present context, I would like to deal briefly with the doxological
dimension of *theology*. The relation between prayer and theology is not
without tension, either historically or existentially. Some of the most ardent
prayer-movements of church history were characterized by far-reaching
mistrust of academic theology. And academic theology resisted, with some
good reasons, the invitations to mix up *pia desideria* with the implacable
search for scientific truth. From both sides, with different options and accents, it was emphasized that prayer is a movement of the heart, whereas
theology is a conceptual exercise, a scientific effort open to objective testing
and publicly presented. Can we honestly combine the two? Might not the
attempt to bring them together merely result in threatening the identity of
both and in alienating them?

The questions are seriously to be considered. I personally think that it is
possible and even necessary to relate the two. I do so not from natural incli-
nation (I am not a particularly "pious type"). I do so rather from my own
ecclesial background, that of the Czech Reformation, which (culminating in
Comenius) strongly emphasized the connection between the personal *praxis
pietatis* and the theological engagement in church and society. Above all, the
doxological character of theological endeavor emerges for me from my theological orientation and conviction. I am convinced that the specific feature
of theological work, not simply in contrast to other scholarly pursuits but
with a notable difference of accent, lies in its attempt to take both the doxological and the methodological elements into account and to bring them
into cooperation. Theology is the thinking side of faith. Here the two elements are combined, though admittedly not without tension.

[20] Müller, "Gebet," pp. 91-93.
[21] I tried to deal with these three dimensions of glorification in my book, *The Theology of
Praise* (Atlanta: John Knox Press, 1982), pp. 48-52.

An old maxim of theological work points in this direction: *Lex orandi—lex credendi* (the law of praying is the law of believing; we might also add that it is the law of thinking and of living). It is the basic law, or, better, the basic movement of theological existence. The formula occurs in Augustine and in such great medieval theologians as Anselm and Aquinas. It also occurs in the Reformers. It relates first the theological enterprise to the church's liturgy. What takes place in worship is not something solemn but theologically unrewarding and irrelevant. The liturgy does not take place outside theological reflection even though it transcends the conceptual. Conversely, as thinkers of the Eastern Orthodox tradition keep reminding us in ecumenical conversations, theology takes place in the context of liturgy. It is itself a liturgical matter, though it has at the same time to discharge other functions, for example, the task of rational wrestling with the truth entrusted to it, and the task of communicating it on the Areopagus of the day. Linking dogmatic deliberations to prayer does not entail the leap into another genre. It is not an impermissible sidestep.

There is a hermeneutical aspect to this affinity between theology and doxology. If it is biblically true that God in Christ, the Triune God, cannot be legitimately approached in a neutral, objectivistic way but only in acts of faith and adoration, then even theology is hardly possible without doxological elements in its deliberations and formulations. This applies to theology as a specific science. "Theology is possible as science exactly and only . . . as theology of a praying faith."[22] Edmund Schlink was right when he spoke emphatically of the "doxological structure of the dogma."[23] I was strengthened in such doxological orientation by the theologians to whom I am most indebted: Josef L. Hromadka of Prague, Karl Barth of Basel, Emil Brunner of Zürich, and the Reformers (not forgetting the impulses of my American friends like James I. McCord, David Willis-Watkins, and Geoffrey Wainwright).[24] Particularly Karl Barth impressed me in this respect. It was no accident that at the head of his early dogmatic lectures in Göttingen in 1924 Barth placed the prayer of Thomas Aquinas: "Merciful God, I ask that thou wilt grant me, as thou pleasest, to seek earnestly, to investigate carefully, to

[22] H. Ott, "Theologie als Gebet und als Wissenschaft," *Theologische Zeitschrift* 14 (1958): 122.

[23] E. Schlink, *Ökumenische Dogmatik: Grundzuge* (Göttingen: Vandenhoeck & Ruprecht, 1983), pp. 64ff.

[24] I refer particularly to the basic work by G. Wainwright, *Doxology: The Praise of God in Worship, Doctrine and Life* (New York: Oxford University Press, 1980); and also to D. Willis, *Daring Prayer* (Atlanta: John Knox Press, 1977).

know truthfully, and to present perfectly, to the glory of thy name, amen."[25] And it is impressive that his last Basel lectures, *Evangelical Theology: An Introduction*, contain a special chapter on prayer, interpreting it as "the first and basic act of theological work,"[26] manifesting that theology needs not only open windows towards what is happening in the life of the church and the world, but above all the *Oberlicht*, the "light from above."

The study of the Reformers helped me to understand how doxology constitutes a safe foundation of our theology. "Safe" not in the sense of a self-confident *securitas carnis*, as a natural *habitus* or spiritual achievement, but as *certitudo* grounded in the One whom I approach in the spirit of prayer. Unforgettable are the sentences of Luther:

> This is our foundation. The gospel commands us not to look at our own good deeds or perfection but at the God of promise himself, at the Mediator Christ himself. This is how our theology achieves its assurance. We are torn away from ourselves and put outside ourselves, so as not to rely on our own powers, conscience, experience, person, or works, but on that which is outside us, namely on the promise and truth of God which can never deceive us.[27]

We find the same stress in Calvin's persuasive comment on the doxology of the Lord's Prayer:

> This is the firm and tranquil repose of our faith. For if our prayers were to be commended to God by our worth, who would dare even mutter in his presence? Now, however miserable we may be, though unworthiest of all, however devoid of all commendation, we will never lack a reason to pray, never be short of assurance, since his Kingdom, power and glory can never be snatched away from our Father.[28]

Doxology is the promise of theology.

Let me conclude my essay by relating its final part to the first one. There is another saying of Karl Barth in my grateful memory. In his later years we heard from him again and again: "To fold one's hands in prayer is the

[25] K. Barth, *The Göttingen Dogmatics: Instruction in the Christian Religion*, ed. H. Reiffen (Grand Rapids: Wm. B. Eerdmans Publishing Co., 1990), vol. 1, p. 3.

[26] Barth, *Evangelical Theology: An Introduction* (Grand Rapids: Wm. B. Eerdmans Publishing Co., 1963), p. 160.

[27] M. Luther, "In epistolam S. Pauli ad Galatas Commentarius," in *D. Martin Luthers Werke: Kritische Gesamtausgabe* (Weimar: Hermann Böhlaus Nachfolger, 1911), vol. 40, pt. 1, p. 585.

[28] Calvin, *Institutes*, vol. 2, pp. 915-916 (III.20.47).

beginning of an uprising against the disorder of the world." The sentence has two foci. It is important not to miss its second part. It counteracts the suspicion that prayer is a substitute for responsible action. We saw that this suspicion (unfortunately too often justified by the behavior of Christians) is one of the main reasons for the loss of credibility of prayer in our secularized world. Here our theology of prayer and our life of prayer are challenged.[29] Prayer is at the heart of Christian faith, but that heart does not beat for itself. It is the source, the beginning of a life of discipleship concerned about the "disorder of the world," and ready to rise up to struggle with it.

This throws a challenging light on all our deliberations about prayer in our time. Our petitions, our struggle for personal identity, cannot be "religious" only, a matter of "metaphysics and inwardness" (to quote Bonhoeffer once more); they concern all matters of our personal life. Our intercessions cannot remain verbal operations; they lead towards a life in solidarity with our neighbors near and far away, particularly with those underprivileged and discriminated against. Our doxology is not a matter of liturgical behavior in the technical sense but the process of *leitourgia* in all realms and relations of life: the beginning of an uprising against the disorder of the world—in and around us.

At the same time, the first part of Barth's sentence, the "to fold the hands in prayer," has to be considered in its full weight. Our struggle for renewal, our Christian life is under promise if we do not forget that the final hope for overcoming the disorder of the world is in God's commitment in the Spirit of Christ, not in our plans and achievements. Thus prayer clarifies and strengthens our engagements. Without it, without the joy of God ("The chief end of human life is to glorify God and to *enjoy him forever*"), our discipleship and our activism become joyless and legalistic labor—and thus counterproductive.

The old monastic wisdom is valid: *Orare et laborare* are the two, irreplaceable foci of Christian life. A Christian needs both—praying and drumming.

[29] A broader exposition of a "theology of prayer" is presented in my book, *The Lord's Prayer*, trans. G. W. Bromiley (Grand Rapids: Wm. B. Eerdmans Publishing Co., 1991). The major parts of the present essay are based on that work.

Enthroned on the Praises and Laments of Israel

by SAMUEL E. BALENTINE

M Y ASSIGNMENT in this symposium, prayer in the Hebrew Bible, is a rather daunting one, involving a large body of information. Typically, discussions of Hebraic prayer have concentrated on the Psalms, a collection of poetic "prayer texts" traditionally associated with the ritual and worship of ancient Israel. In recent studies we have been urged to expand our horizons beyond the Psalms to include a significant number of other prayers which are embedded within the narrative contexts of the Hebrew scriptures. To cite but one example, M. Greenberg has identified some 97 prose texts where the words of prayers are recorded.[1] When we include texts where the *act* of prayer is mentioned, but the words are not recorded, then the number of references swells considerably. And if we think of prayer as communication with God not only in *words* but also through *acts*, then we should recognize that also to be included among our resources is a variety of nonverbal approaches to God, e.g., sacrifice, dance, ritual gestures with the body, any one of which may impart, through the performative act, information to the deity.[2]

In this presentation I focus on prayer as words, more specifically on the texts which record this special speech directed from people to God. As an introduction to prayer in this restricted sense, we may understand that the words of prayer preserved in the Hebrew Bible fall generally into two broad categories: praise and lament. As C. Westermann has observed, "In Israel all speaking to God moves between these two poles."[3]

In the Hebrew Bible both praise and lament are authentic and necessary expressions of faith. Both responses are directed to God as offerings of trust and commitment. Even in suffering, when God may seem more absent than present, prayer is addressed to the elusive God. So it is that even in lamen-

---

[1] M. Greenberg, *Biblical Prose Prayer As a Window to the Popular Religion of Ancient Israel* (Berkeley, Los Angeles, and London: University of California Press, 1983). For the list of these texts see pp. 59-60.

[2] On the distinction between prayer as *text* and prayer as *act*, see the helpful discussion of S. D. Gill, "Prayer," in *The Encyclopedia of Religion*, ed. M. Eliade (New York: Macmillan Publishing Company, 1987), vol. 11, pp. 489-494.

[3] C. Westermann, *Praise and Lament in the Psalms* (Atlanta: John Knox Press, 1981), p. 154. See further his *Elements of Old Testament Theology* (Atlanta: John Knox Press, 1982), p. 156; *The Living Psalms* (Grand Rapids: William B. Eerdmans Publishing Co., 1989), pp. 10-11.

tation, the affirmation may go forth that God remains "enthroned on the praises of Israel" (Ps. 22:3).

In the pages that follow I propose to track Hebrew prayers of praise and lament in both their psalmic and narrative contexts. It is my contention that both these contexts are informative and essential for understanding the *form* as well as the *function* of such prayers in the faith of ancient Israel. I will conclude with some theological observations concerning the legacy of Hebraic prayer for the contemporary community of faith.

As preface to our investigation of these matters, however, I turn first to an important issue which I believe necessarily shapes our ultimate understanding of prayer in the Hebrew Bible. As communication which offers to God both praise and lament, prayer is inherently a human activity. Yet such communication, we must remember, is always directed explicitly to God. It is appropriate therefore to begin our exploration of these human words by reflecting on the nature of the God to whom they are directed. What is it about the nature and character of God that both summons forth and enables the response of prayer?

I. The God of Prayer

"In the beginning God"—with these words the Hebrew Bible presents a confessional perspective that shapes all that follows. By whatever criteria prayer is defined, it also, perhaps especially, is shaped by this confession. All prayer is directed to God.

When speaking of God, the Hebrew Bible almost always resorts to the language of metaphor, principally to metaphors drawn from the human sphere which serve to anchor the image of God in human experience. Specific to our focus here are those metaphors that promote an understanding of the divine-human relationship as dialogic.[4] God is portrayed as *speaking* and acting toward humanity, and *listening* for, hence inviting human response. People listen and receive a word from God, and offer speech and action in response. While such metaphors are clearly not to be taken literally, they do serve, nevertheless, to depict a reality about God and God's preferred model of relationship with humanity.[5] In Hebrew scripture these are "controlling" metaphors.[6] Wherever God is being God and humanity is acting in full accord with divine intentions, God and people are in dialogue

---

[4] On the importance of metaphorical language for the Bible's portrait of God, see especially T. Fretheim, *The Suffering of God* (Philadelphia: Fortress Press, 1984), chaps. 1-3.

[5] On "reality depiction" as a function of religious metaphorical language see J. M. Soskice, *Metaphor and Religious Language* (Oxford: Clarendon Press, 1985), pp. 97-117.

[6] Cf. Fretheim, *Suffering of God*, pp. 11-12.

one with another. "In the beginning God," and from the beginning God is portrayed as desiring not only to speak and act and control, but also to listen and consider and respond.

This dialogue between God and humanity involves a genuine partnership. The Hebrew Bible presents this partnership as a covenant relationship. God is committed to Israel and requires moral conduct befitting the divine intention for a holy people. The people of Israel are committed to the one God Adonai and pledge obedience to divine instructions for life and worship. In return for their covenant faithfulness, the people expect reciprocal fidelity from the holy, sovereign One. Certainly this covenant partnership involves an unequal distribution of power. God is the initiator of the covenant, not Israel. Even so, both parties commit themselves to responsibility for the maintenance of the partnership. It cannot be sustained in its fullest form by either party alone.

The central point is that covenant partnership is fundamentally dialogical. Two parties are mutually bound to one another in a relationship that is desirable and important for both. Both parties have a voice and a role to play, and neither can disregard the appeals of the other and maintain the relationship as it is intended to be. If either God or Israel does not lend its voice to the dialogue, then communication fails and the relationship is impoverished by distance and silence.[7]

Let me sharpen this point with respect to the discourse of prayer. Covenant partnership means that God chooses not to utilize the divine prerogatives of power to reduce Israel's response to submission or silence or monotones of praise. Such limitations on human response would effectively eviscerate genuine relationship, substituting instead enforced obedience or passive devotion. Covenant partnership also means that Israel cannot and does not withhold from God the full range of human experience. Joy and suffering, prosperity and deprivation, communion and confrontation, all characterize life in covenant relationship with God. Without the sharing of this full range of human experience, what I have referred to broadly as praise and lament, partnership risks becoming only a veneer for tacit understandings which have no real claim on either party.

II. Prayer in the Context of the Psalms

What then are the words of praise and lament that are directed toward this responsive God? Here I focus on the forms of praise and lament prayers

[7] See especially T. Fretheim, "Prayer in the Old Testament: Creating Space in the World for God," in A Primer on Prayer, ed. P. Sponheim (Philadelphia: Fortress Press, 1988), pp. 51-62.

in the Hebrew Bible with a view towards understanding their function in the faith of Israel. In this presentation I cannot give a full survey of the history of the discussion. Let me begin simply by acknowledging that for the better part of this century, the study of biblical prayer has been hardly distinguishable from the study of the Psalms.

With the pioneering work of H. Gunkel and S. Mowinckel on the Psalms, form criticism began to play the lead role methodologically in identifying psalms/prayers of praise and lament.[8] So influential has their work been that in the ensuing years most of our efforts have been directed towards refining their proposals in two areas, namely the *forms* of these prayers and their *settings*.

With respect to the forms of praise and lament no one has contributed more significantly to this discussion than C. Westermann. Westermann has proposed a distinction between what he terms "descriptive" and "narrative" praise.[9] Both types of praise exhibit in essence a similar structure: 1) an introduction/summons to praise; 2) a main body setting forth the reasons for praise; and 3) a concluding word of praise. What distinguishes these two types of praise is the *reason* for praise. "Narrative" praise typically recounts God's past acts of deliverance, usually in concrete and specific terms. Thus praise is offered in response to *what God has done* (e.g., Ps. 30:4-10). "Descriptive" praise, on the other hand, is the praise appropriate to worship where the reason for praising God is more liturgically expressed, that is, more abstractly expressed, in terms of God's inherent majesty and goodness (e.g., Ps. 146:5-10a).

Concerning lament psalms, Westermann has emphasized a typical structure consisting of three essential components: invocation, lament, petition.[10] Especially influential has been Westermann's suggestion that these structural features evidence a sequenced movement within the prayer from lament to appeal, that is, from suffering to confidence that a reversal of fortunes can be forthcoming (e.g., Ps. 13:5). Such a movement indicates that lament's concern is not primarily with the portrayal of suffering, but with its removal or alleviation. In Westermann's words, "lamentation has no meaning in and of itself." So it is that "there is not a single Psalm of lament that stops with lamentation."[11] Rather every lament functions as an appeal.[12]

---

[8] The seminal works are H. Gunkel and J. Begrich, *Einleitung in die Psalmen*, 3d ed. (Göttingen: Vandenhoeck & Ruprecht, 1966); S. Mowinckel, *Psalmenstudien*, 6 vols. (Kristiania: Jacob Dybwad, 1921-1924); cf. S. Mowinckel, *The Psalms in Israel's Worship*, 2 vols. (Oxford: Basil Blackwell, 1962).

[9] Westermann, *Praise and Lament*, pp. 52-162.

[10] Ibid., pp. 165-213.

[11] Ibid., p. 266; cf. *Elements of Old Testament Theology*, p. 169.

With respect to the life settings of psalmic prayers, Gunkel and Mo-winckel both stressed a "cultic" or worship setting, though they differed in important ways on how they understood this. Since their work, considerable attention has focused on clarifying what should be understood by the term "cultic." The most stimulating and provocative suggestions have come from E. Gerstenberger. Gerstenberger has argued that the settings of the Psalms can be more adequately defined from a sociological perspective.[13] Specifically he has identified two main social settings within which religious rituals are normally used: 1) small, primary groups of family, neighborhood, or community, where ritual patterns are largely spontaneous; and 2) larger, secondary organizations where membership is anonymous and administration is bureaucratic, e.g., the temple. In these secondary, institutional settings ritual patterns are formalized and centralized in accordance with the needs and interests of the nation or state. Broadly speaking, Gerstenberger locates psalms of lamentation in the small, primary group settings, where ad hoc services are occasioned by specific circumstances, e.g., draught, military defeat. Psalms of praise he situates in the larger, secondary, institutional setting where seasonal and life-span rituals are regularly celebrated.[14]

My interest is not in detailing the history of Psalm research, to whose scope and complexity the above survey hardly does justice. Rather, I want only to suggest two things. First, with respect to the Psalms, biblical scholarship has only seldom moved beyond the fundamental questions of form and setting posed originally by Gunkel and Mowinckel. There have been some notable exceptions, particularly in the work of Westermann[15] and W. Brueggemann,[16] but in the main we have yet to address in any compre-

---

[12] As E. S. Gerstenberger has observed, laments are complaints in the fullest sense of the word, *Anklagen* not *Klagen*, that is, statements of protest, not of resignation or submission. See "Jeremiah's Complaints: Observations on Jer. 15:10-21," *Journal of Biblical Literature* 82 (1963): 393-408.

[13] E. S. Gerstenberger, *Der bittende Mensch* (Neukirchen: Neukirchener Verlag, 1980), pp. 113-168; *Psalms, Part 1; With an Introduction to Cultic Poetry* (Grand Rapids: William B. Eerdmans Publishing Co., 1988), pp. 30-34.

[14] Gerstenberger, *Psalms*, pp. 9-19. See further R. Albertz (*Persönliche Frömmigkeit und offizielle Religion* [Stuggart: Calwer Verlag, 1978], pp. 23-96), who has followed Gerstenberger by contrasting the personal piety emerging out of the *Kleinkult*, the small group setting, with the official religion of secondary, institutionalized piety.

[15] Particularly helpful have been Westermann's discussion of the theological importance of blessing (*Blessing in the Bible and the Life of the Church* [Philadelphia: Fortress Press, 1978]) and lament ("The Role of Lament in the Theology of the Old Testament," *Interpretation* 28 [1974]: 20-38 [= *Praise and Lament*, pp. 259-280]). For an idea of how such themes contribute to the larger picture of the theology of the Hebrew Bible see *Elements of Old Testament Theology*, pp. 153-216.

[16] Note especially "Psalms and the Life of Faith: A Suggested Typology of Function," *Journal for the Study of the Old Testament* 17 (1980): 3-32; *The Message of the Psalms* (Minne-

hensive way the *function* of the psalms as prayers in the life and worship of ancient Israel.

Secondly, we may note that the study of prayer, in the context of the Psalms, has largely been defined by form-critical concerns, particularly the question of form. The enduring influence of the form-critical approach on biblical prayer is evident in what are arguably the three most important books on "prayer in the Old Testament" published in the last 60 years.

In the work of A. Wendel (1931), L. Krinetzki (1965), and H. G. Reventlow (1986) biblical prayer is defined and interpreted primarily in relation to the Psalms.[17] Krinetzki and Reventlow both employ form-critical distinctions to identify and isolate *prayers* of praise and *prayers* of lament, and in both cases their examples of such prayers are drawn almost exclusively from the Psalter.[18]

Wendel concentrates on the prose prayers of Genesis-2 Kings, prayers he determines to be "free" from the cultic sphere of institutionalized worship. Even so, the *prose* prayers he isolates are defined in accordance with the form-critical designations of Psalms' *Gattungen*. In essence Wendel treats these prose prayers like the Psalms, as if their narrative context were non-existent, or as if such a context did not seriously affect their meaning.

We may conclude that the form-critical approach to biblical prayer has been both productive and non-productive. On the positive side, discussion of the form and general setting of psalm prayers has progressed to a level of sophistication and discernment heretofore unparalleled. This represents solid achievement and is not to be undervalued. Yet, negatively, we have given inadequate attention to a significant number of other prayer texts, namely those in prose contexts. On the one hand, to speak of prayer has become virtually synonymous with speaking of the Psalms. On the other hand, prose prayers which have been addressed solely through the lens of form criticism, with its inherent tendency to standardize and categorize, have been robbed of the one element of their literary setting that distinguishes them from the Psalms—their narrative context.

---

apolis: Augsburg Press, 1984); *Abiding Astonishment: Psalms, Modernity, and the Making of History* (Louisville: Westminster/John Knox Press, 1991).

[17] A. Wendel, *Das freie Laiengebet im vorexilischen Israel* (Leipzig: Verlag von Eduard Pfeiffer, 1931); L. Krinetzki, *Israels Gebet im Alten Testament* (Aschaffenburg: Paul Pattloch Verlag, 1965); H. G. Reventlow, *Gebet im Alten Testament* (Stuttgart, Berlin, Köln, and Mainz: W. Kohlhammer, 1986).

[18] Reventlow addresses the prose prayers which occur outside the Psalter, for example, the intercessory prayers of the prophets, or the post-exilic prayers of penitence in Ezra 9, Nehemiah 9, and Daniel 9. But in his judgment such prayers derive from and remain dependent on the cultic tradition of prayer represented in the Psalms.

III. Prayer in the Context of Narrative

Interestingly, it has been C. Westermann's own form-critical clarifications concerning praise and lament psalms that have provided a foundation for a new stage in the study of biblical prayer. Westermann has recognized that psalmic prayers have both a historical antecedent and a sequel in the prose prayers of the Hebrew Bible. In his proposed outline of the development of prayer, the Psalms are understood to be representative of the historical mid-point.

To be specific, Westermann distinguishes three stages in the history of prayer.[19] In the earliest stage he identifies brief addresses to God which arise directly and naturally from situations in daily life. Such prayers, expressing lament (e.g., Judg. 15:18; 21:3), petition (e.g., 2 Sam. 15:31), or praise (e.g., Ex. 18:10) typically occur in narrative or prose contexts and are presented as constitutive parts of the recounted course of events. The occasion for these prayers requires no cultic framework, the pray-er no liturgical assistance.

In the second or middle stage of prayer's development, these short calls to God come together in the formal structures of psalms. Units of once independent, brief prayers come together in poetic compositions which then become vehicles for worship. In this poeticized form, a psalm takes up the real experiences of specific individuals and transforms them into prayers for the worshiping congregation which are suitable for transmission from one generation to the next. The undergirding societal structure that makes such worship possible and such prayer desirable is the settled life secured by the monarchy and the state. With the temple as the central religious center for the state, psalms encourage a worship orientation which Westermann suggests is characterized by a "double movement." Worshipers are summoned from their own homes to the "house of God," and then from the worship service back into their own homes and work.[20]

With the dissolution of the monarchy and the end of worship in the temple, prayer enters a third stage in its developmental process. In the long prose prayers of 1 Kings 8, Ezra 9, and Nehemiah 9, prayer undergoes a transformation with respect to both style and content. Stylistically there is a shift from poetry to prose, commensurate, in Westermann's opinion, with

---

[19] Westermann's initial delineation of these stages appears in "Gebet II: Im AT," in *Die Religion in Geschichte und Gegenwart*, ed. K. Galling (Tübingen: J. C. B. Mohr, Paul Siebeck, 1958), vol. 2, pp. 1213-1217. In Westermann's subsequent discussions of the history of prayer, his position remains essentially unchanged. Cf. *Elements of Old Testament Theology*, pp. 154-156; *Living Psalms*, pp. 13-16.

[20] Westermann, *Elements of Old Testament Theology*, p. 155.

the loss of the self-evident membership in the community of faith which the temple had nurtured, and its replacement by a "conscious and reflected belonging."[21]

With respect to content, Westermann observes that praise and lament prayers gradually lose their distinctives as independent addresses to God. In their place emerges a new form of prayer in which, for the first time, praise serves as the preface to expressions of penitence and petitions for divine forgiveness. This new combination of praise preceding petition represents a fundamental change in the understanding of prayer in the late biblical period.[22] It is a change which Westermann associates with the trauma of the post-exilic period when concern for the righteousness of God emerges as such a predominant issue, that the lament or the complaint against God recedes more and more into the background.[23]

I should pause here for a moment to offer one further observation which will be important for our focus on the Lord's Prayer in this symposium. The practice of praise preceding petition, which emerges in Israel after the exile, has a long and important history. This way of praying can be traced through a variety of late biblical and post-biblical texts. It is even more pronounced in the statutory prayers of the synagogue which take shape between the first and fifth centuries C.E.[24] Here we may refer to the Talmudic dictum: "Let a man always declare the praise of God and afterwards present his petition" (B. Berakhot 32a). The prayer *par excellence* which displays this praise-petition pattern is, of course, the "Prayer of Eighteen Benedictions."

We will explore in this symposium, I am sure, the linkage betweeen the form of Jesus' model prayer and the genre of Jewish statutory prayer. Both follow a basic pattern of praise plus petition. While there are important differences between Jesus' prayer and synagogue prayer, with respect to *form*, the Lord's Prayer appears to be modelled on its Jewish antecedent.[25] Westermann's analysis of the development of biblical prayer enables us to see more clearly that this pattern of praise and petition has roots in the later stages of ancient Israel's history.

---

[21] Ibid., p. 156.

[22] Cf. Westermann, *Living Psalms*, pp. 15-16.

[23] On the "late history of lament" see especially Westermann, *Praise and Lament*, pp. 201-212.

[24] E.g., Qumran psalms, Psalms of Solomon (e.g., 18:1-5), and 4 Ezra. For discussion of these and other texts see Westermann, *Praise and Lament*, pp. 204-212.

[25] Cf. J. Heinemann, *Prayer in the Talmud* (Berlin, New York: Walter de Gruyter, 1977), p. 191. See further Heinemann's more general discussion in "The Background of Jesus' Prayer in the Jewish Liturgical Tradition," in *The Lord's Prayer and Jewish Liturgy*, ed. J. J. Petuchowski and M. Brocke (New York: Seabury Press, 1978), pp. 81-92.

To return to our present focus, Westermann's survey of the development of biblical prayer calls attention to the deficiency of previous studies which have offered a simplistic equation of prayer and the Psalms. A one-sided preoccupation with the Psalms affords at best an understanding of but one stage of prayer's development. For a more comprehensive picture, we must address that significant other collection of prayers which are preserved for us in the Hebrew Bible, namely the prayers embedded in narrative contexts.

In recent years we have begun to explore the structure and function of nonpsalmic prayers and hence to broaden our theological discernment concerning Hebraic prayer.[26] Particularly instructive has been M. Greenberg's suggestion that it is the nonpsalmic prayers of the Hebrew Bible, i.e., prayers embedded in narrative contexts, that provide a unique understanding of Israel's religious life. He contends that the Psalms are inadequate for this task precisely because they reveal so little concrete information about the speaker of the prayer, the situation in which the prayer is delivered, or the outcome for the pray-er. It is just here that "embedded" prayers have an advantage. Prose prayers are set within particular life situations where putative authors/speakers are supplied by the narrative context. Embedded within a narrative context, prayer plays an integral role in delineating character, in unfolding the drama of a sequence of events, and in influencing the outcome of the narrative circumstances in which it is used.[27]

Let me illustrate the advantage of this new emphasis on prayer within narrative contexts with but two brief examples. The first is a piece of poetic praise, framed by a surrounding narrative in such a way that its generalized liturgical rhetoric is in effect concretized by the particularities of its literary

---

[26] A number of studies have called attention to the genetic connection between intrahuman speech patterns and the ritual patterns of psalmic speech. See Gerstenberger, *Der bittende Mensch*, pp. 17-63; Greenberg, *Biblical Prose Prayer*, pp. 19-37; A. Aejmelaeus, *The Traditional Prayer in the Psalms* (New York and Berlin: Walter de Gruyter, 1986), pp. 88-91. There are basic modes of speech between humans that inform the special discourse of prayer. We may note, for example, the similarities between petitionary prayer and petitionary speech to a king. Cf. Greenberg, *Biblical Prose Prayer*, pp. 22-24; R. N. Boyce, *The Cry to God in the Old Testament* (Atlanta: Scholars Press, 1988), pp. 27-40.

Such studies make it clear that prayer is not an invention of the cult or ritual experts, to which people must adjust upon entering the sphere of worship. Rather, common speech patterns expressing joy and distress grow out of everyday life and, as such, precede and inform cultic language.

[27] Greenberg, *Biblical Prose Prayer*, pp. 1-18. Greenberg recognizes that the tendency has been to treat prose prayers as *mere* literary creations, i.e., as literary artifacts that do not provide direct or immediate witness to what actually happened. While he grants that all prayer texts have been shaped by authors and narrators, he argues that this does not automatically consign them to the ranks of the inauthentic. In his words, "even if it is granted that the prayers are not veridical, that does not foreclose their being verisimilar" (p. 8).

setting. The second example is a prose prayer of lament, reminiscent of lament psalms, which in its context serves to shape the surrounding narrative in intentional ways.

The first example is the well known Song of Hannah in 1 Sam. 2:1-10.[28] A general consensus has long held that this song is secondary in its present context. The arguments in support of this judgment are well known and need not be reviewed here. We may note simply that the language of the song is highly metaphorical and figurative and in many respects would appear to have little or no concrete relevance for the particular circumstances of the Hannah narrative.[29] If, for example, the song is excerpted from its narrative setting, its form and content would identify it as a typical song of thanksgiving from an anonymous pray-er. Like other thanksgiving songs in the Psalter, this song could be appropriated by a number of different persons, in a variety of situations, for different reasons. The psalm with which it is most often compared is Psalm 113.[30]

In its narrative context, however, this general song of thanks is particularized by identification specifically with the circumstances of Hannah. No longer is it the prayer of just anyone, it is in this setting specifically the prayer of Hannah, wife of Elkanah of the city of Ramathaim. Now it is not a prayer of *general* thanksgiving, unattached to the specifics which call it forth; it is a prayer of gratitude offered on the specific occasion of once-barren Hannah's conception of the child for whom she had petitioned (cf. 1:10-11). Now the otherwise general references in vv. 4-10 to the reversal of fortunes experienced by the feeble and the hungry, the barren and the poor, become focused on the particular change in Hannah's status occasioned by the birth of the boy Samuel. In sum, the narrative context serves to "literalize" poetic metaphor.[31] In so doing, the narrative has preserved—perhaps

[28] For other examples of poetic praise within narrative contexts see Ex. 15:1-18, Judg. 5:1-31, 2 Sam. 22:2-31, Deut. 32:1-43, Is. 38:9-20, Jon. 2:1-9.

[29] E.g., it is not clear how the reference to the "bows of the mighty" bears directly on the life of barren and plaintive Hannah. On the other hand, where stereotypical language does make connection with Hannah's situation, it is clear that the song cannot be taken simply as a literal representation of the facts. For example, the song refers to the barren woman "who has borne seven" (v. 5), but according to the narrative Hannah had only *six* children (cf. 2:21).

[30] E.g. J. T. Willis, "The Song of Hannah and Psalm 113," *Catholic Biblical Quarterly* 35 (1973): 139-154. See further R. Polzin's analysis of the similarities to Psalm 18 [= 2 Samuel 22]. In his view, Hannah's song is an artful abbreviation of David's final hymn of praise, the two poems forming a poetic *inclusio* for the Deuteronomist's history of kingship (*Samuel and the Deuteronomist: A Literary Study of the Deuteronomic History, Part Two: 1 Samuel* [San Francisco: Harper and Row, 1989], pp. 31-36).

[31] Cf. P. Miller's observations concerning the "literalization" of poetic laments which have been embedded within narrative contexts, "Trouble and Woe: Interpreting the Biblical Laments," *Interpretation* 37 (1983): 32-45.

we should say restored—the essential connection between *praise* and the *reason for praise* that characterizes the simplest and earliest forms of praise in the Hebrew Bible.[32]

A second example of prayer within a narrative context I take from a collection of prose prayers which focus on the petition for divine justice: Gen. 18:22-33; Ex. 32:7-14; Num. 11:4-34; Num. 14:11-25; Josh. 7:7-9; 1 Kings. 17:17-24.[33] These texts in all likelihood derive from different historical settings. Nevertheless, we may discern in them a common rhetorical pattern. Each of these texts functions within a literary context that has three essential features: 1) some crisis in the relationship between pray-er and God; 2) a response to the crisis in the form of a prayer which raises questions about divine justice and/or divine intentions; 3) some resolution or at least explanation of the crisis which, within the narrative context, is presented as the result of the pray-er's discourse with God. Simply stated, these texts all revolve around the themes of crisis, prayer, resolution of crisis. We may illustrate further by looking specifically at Num. 14:11-25.

The literary context of Moses' prayer in Numbers 14 is complicated. We note simply that a Priestly framework provides the themes of sin (vv. 1-10) and divine judgment (vv. 26-38). It is striking, however, that this Priestly frame is "interrupted" precisely at the point where one would expect the judgment to be announced. The judgment is in fact delayed to allow for the unfolding of a rather lengthy address from Moses to God which has been inserted in vv. 11-25.[34] In this address fundamental questions concerning God's intentions are raised, a petition for God's forgiveness is presented, and an assurance of God's forgiveness is received. As noted above, the components of this prayer—lament, petition, assurance—are typical in lament psalms. When the narrative returns to report the expected word of judgment from God, the reader/hearer has been prepared to receive it as a judgment tempered with divine compassion and limited by divine commitment to justice and fairness. This literary sequencing of the events may be illustrated as follows.

[32] Westermann has argued that in its "most original and immediate form," Israel's praise follows a basic structure of praise plus reason for praise. See *Praise and Lament*, pp. 87-90.

[33] I have discussed these texts in more detail in "Prayer in the Wilderness Traditions: In Pursuit of Divine Justice," *Hebrew Annual Review* 9 (1985): 53-74 and "Prayers for Justice in the Old Testament: Theodicy and Theology," *Catholic Biblical Quarterly* 51 (1989): 597-616.

[34] These verses are commonly taken as supplementary material, though opinion is divided as to their origin. See my discussion in "Prayer in the Wilderness Traditions," pp. 66-71.

vv. 1-10 The congregation's rebellion against the leadership of Moses and Aaron. They move to stone them . . . and the glory of the LORD appears at the tent of meeting.

vv. 11-25 Moses' intervention with petition for forgiveness (*slḥ*). God forgives (*slḥ*) according to Moses' request *and* punishes.

vv. 26-38 "And the LORD said to Moses and Aaron . . ." Divine judgment pronounced.

To summarize, the composite narrative of Numbers 14 is in agreement that disloyal behavior in the wilderness resulted in God's punishment. But in its final form the text attributes this judgment to a God who both judges and forgives, a God who can be addressed and moved to show mercy to a guilty people. In its final form the narrative assigns to Moses' prayer a position of major importance. Positioned between the announcement of punishment and the execution of that punishment, the prayer occurs at precisely the point of literary climax and from this point determines the final outcome of the situation.

What is particularly noteworthy about the prayers in 1 Sam. 2:1-10 and Num. 14:11-25 is that both appear to have been *edited into* a literary context. In both cases the result is a portrait of God and humanity dialoguing with one another over matters that count. Both praise and petition, both thankfulness and lamentation are presented as authentic responses to concrete experiences in life. As these texts help us to understand, such responses to God are not found *only* in the formal context of temple worship.

IV. THE LEGACY OF HEBREW PRAYER

I have suggested that the prayers of the Hebrew Bible present both praise and lament as authentic expressions of faith. In the combined witness of narrative and psalmic prayers we are invited to understand something of the "double movement" in the dialogue between God and humanity of which Westermann has spoken.[35] On the one hand worshipers are summoned from the particularities of daily situations to the house of God, where liturgical discourse gathers up individual responses into collective offerings of the community of faith. On the other hand, liturgical discourse offers

---

[35] See Westermann, *Elements of Old Testament Theology*, p. 155.

"patterned prayer-speech"[36] that may be freely fitted to specific circumstances. In other words, in the narrative of life as in the liturgy of the temple, prayers of praise and lament represent the two-way traffic between heaven and earth. Such discourse, I submit, is the quintessential dialogue of faith where God and humanity work in partnership to maintain covenant relationship.

I suggest that both the church and the synagogue are summoned to a ministry that promotes and enables this dialogue. Let me comment briefly on but two responsibilities bequeathed to us all by this legacy of praise and lament.

First, one important ministry of the practice of praise is the affirmation that in *all* of life's experiences there is a transcendent reality.[37] To praise God is to acknowledge that life is a gift from God. It is to affirm that we cannot create of our own resources the real joys of life. We cannot will them into existence either by our faith or our technology. Life and the joy that fills it are gifts from the creator. It is the ministry of praise to *keep us in God*, that is, to keep the community mindful of the transcendent dimension in life. When all of life is received as a gift, then we submit willingly to the requirement to live with a deep sense of gratitude, genuine honesty, and profound responsibility. The church and the synagogue must be at work in the world through the ministry of praise to *shape the future of people and institutions* in accordance with this transcendent reality and its demands.

To put the edge on this point, we might ask what would be the loss for church and synagogue, for all communities of faith, for the world in which we live, if we do not practice the ministry of praise? I suggest two "costly losses"[38] should we neglect this ministry.

(1) Without the summons to praise, it is likely that our natural bent towards narcissism will turn us inward rather than upward. We will languish in a stupor of self-intoxication. The realization of the transcendent God will fade. In its place will be the gods we have made with our own hands, and they will look like us. Our lives and our institutions (including our religious institutions), our communities and our world, will be one step closer to yielding to the ultimate idolatry, viz., self-deification. In this sense, the summons to praise is a summons to obedience to the first commandment. It is a

[36] Cf. Greenberg, *Biblical Prose Prayer*, p. 15

[37] On prayer as a vital link between everyday life and the transcendent realm, see Greenberg, *Biblical Prose Prayer*, pp. 51-52.

[38] W. Brueggemann has used this term with respect to prayers of lament in "The Costly Loss of Lament," *Journal for the Study of the Old Testament* 36 (1986): 57-71. The term is no less appropriate, I submit, with reference to the importance of praise prayer.

summons to love God and God alone. It is therefore a summons radically subversive of self-love or mindless allegiance to other persons or institutions.[39]

(2) If the church and the synagogue do not practice the ministry of praise, they will forfeit the role of celebrating, and hence proclaiming, the freedom and power of God to overturn the status quo. The specific referent here is Hannah's prayer in 1 Samuel 2. However, the point I make is also generally applicable to the larger collection of praise prayers in the Hebrew Bible, where praise is typically anchored in the acknowledgment of who God is and how God has cared for the world and its inhabitants. In Hannah's prayer, the praise offered to God echoes with the remembrance of the reversal of suffering. To participate in such praise is to remain ever mindful that in God's world human impossibilities must yield to the wonderful possibilities of divine reversal.[40] It is to remember, and give thanks, with Hannah that the lowly can be lifted up, the powerful can be brought down. Without the summons to praise both the lowly and the powerful will be tempted to the conclusion that the status is quo, that possibilities unseen are inauthentic and unlikely, that the world's power to define reality is ultimate and unchallenged.[41]

Not only in life's joys and successes but also in its sorrows and failures must the church and the synagogue practice the ministry of prayer. Thus I point to a second responsibility which derives from the legacy of Hebraic lament. I suggest that to follow the Hebraic practice of lamentation is to engage in a radical act of faith that seeks to *shape the future of God*. In essence, one important ministry of the practice of lament is *to keep God in the community and in the world*. We may think of this along the lines proposed by A. Heschel: "To pray means to bring God back into the world ... to expand His presence." Such a task is not only possible, but necessary, for, as Heschel continues, "His being immanent in the world depends on us."[42]

My particular referent here is Moses' prayer in Numbers 14, though again I would submit that the point I make is also valid for prayers of lamentation generally. Moses' address in Numbers 14 illustrates specifically the daring

---

[39] Cf. P. Miller, "In Praise and Thanksgiving," *Theology Today* 45 (1988): 187-188.

[40] On praise as a basic, yet irrational, trust in the endless power of God to surprise, see W. Brueggemann, "The Psalms as Prayer," *Reformed Liturgy and Music* 23 (1989): 19-20.

[41] On praise as a constitutive, transforming act that resists domestication by status quo powers, see W. Brueggemann, *Israel's Praise: Doxology against Idolatry and Ideology* (Philadelphia: Fortress Press, 1988).

[42] A. Heschel, *The Insecurity of Freedom* (New York: Farrar, Straus and Giroux, 1966), p. 258.

work of intercession. The context for his address, as noted above, follows a basic pattern of crisis, prayer, resolution of crisis, so that a crucial role is suggested for prayer in determining the final outcome of the situation.

In short, Moses' prayer is portrayed as having made a difference, not only for the people, but also for God. In this and other such accounts of intercessory prayer, the text invites us to consider the question, "What if Moses (and others) had not prayed?" Would God have stayed in the world, in Moses' case, in covenant relationship with such disobedient followers, if there had been no petition for forgiveness? Of course, we may be inclined to rush quickly past this intercession to answer that God always intended to forgive and relent. And yet, we must remember that this prayer has been edited into a narrative context, as if to force a suspension in our final evaluation until we have considered the dialogue between God and Moses.

We may go on to make one further observation about the ministry of lament. The standard process of lamentation—invocation, lament, petition—serves for Moses and a host of others in the Hebrew Bible to bring before God serious questions concerning suffering and injustice. With thundering questions like "Why?" (e.g., Num. 11:14) and "How long O Lord" (e.g., Ps. 13:1, 2) these pray-ers rail against the inequities of life and the God who allows them . . . or causes them. In this regard, prayers of lament serve as a vehicle for addressing theodicean issues, i.e., issues about God and justice.[43] It is the task of lament not simply to complain to God about injustice, but *to move God to be just*. These are prayers offered in the certain conviction that God must stay in the world as a God of justice. As Abraham's question puts the issue so sharply in Gen. 18:25: "Shall not the Judge of all the earth do justice?"

Again we may address the importance of the ministry of lament with a question. What is to be lost if such praying is neglected or denied? The question may be answered in a variety of ways.[44] Let me offer just one response. It is the very nature of lamentation to resist resignation and to press for change. Where there is lament, there is life, and even in the midst of suffering, this life will be vital and expectant. When the lament ceases to function and all questions are silenced, then what is, is accepted as what will be, in religion, in society, in the political and economic structures of life.

Here we need to be reminded that the denial of suffering is not only a spiritual loss. When lamentation over oppression and suffering, failure and disappointment are forfeited, it is likely that the issues of social and political

---

[43] For further discussion see the references cited above, note 33.
[44] Cf. Brueggemann, "Costly Loss," pp. 60-64.

injustice will also be silenced. The church and the synagogue must know themselves forever constrained by the witness of these lament prayers to promote both *piety* and *justice*, both on *earth* and in *heaven*. As Brueggemann has suggested, if there is silence on justice issues in the sanctuary, eventually these issues are muffled outside the sanctuary as well.[45] If religious institutions acquiesce in this silence, they will cease to minister to the broken and downtrodden. Of greater consequence, when faith is stripped of lament, then the concession is made that suffering and injustice are not only real and hurtful, they are also final.

But we need not make this concession. Indeed we must not. Our Hebraic legacy of prayer summons us toward a different, more radical notion of covenant partnership with God that holds in tension the discourse of praise and lament. This legacy is clearly nurtured and sustained, though not without modification, in the traumatic experience of exile, the re-articulation of Jewish faith in the nascent synagogue, and the emergence of the early church. The details of this long historical development I must now leave to my colleagues in this symposium. For my part I wish to conclude by reaffirming, with the Hebrew Bible, that from the beginning there is God, and from the very beginning, God has been enthroned on the praises and laments of Israel.

[45] Ibid., pp. 63-64. See further W. Brueggemann, "Theodicy in a Social Dimension," *Journal for the Study of the Old Testament* 33 (1985): 3-25.

Jewish Prayers in the Time of Jesus*

by JAMES H. CHARLESWORTH

TODAY we Christians can study Jewish prayer during the time of Jesus without the prejudices and blinders of the past.[1] No longer must we begin our study by striving to correct Emile Schürer's grotesque distortion of Jewish prayer before A.D. 70; surely none of us holds either that in the time of Jesus of Nazareth Jewish prayer was bound in the fetters of a rigid mechanism, or that piety at that time no longer existed among Jews.[2] It is also not necessary to reply to a macabre wayward triumphalism which claims that God does not hear the prayers of Jews; we all agree that this exasperation reflects a betrayal of Christian theology.

No more should it be necessary, moreover, to detract from an appreciation of the essence of Jewish prayer by preoccupying ourselves with the struggle to sail between the Charybdis of anti-Semitism, which replaces Jesus' commandment of love with Satanic hatred, and the Scylla of philo-Semitism, which impairs the integrity of Christian affirmations.

Today we honor Jews who continue to recite prayers which took definitive shape in the Holy Land during the time of Jesus. We enjoy their presence in our collegial gatherings and invite them to teach alongside us here at Princeton Theological Seminary. Chanting the ancient Hebrew with them in a synagogue, to herald the beginning of Sabbath on Friday evening, evokes reflections on the social dynamics of prayer in Nazareth and Capernaum, as Jesus joined other Jews in the celebration of Simhat Torah, the Joy of Torah.

* I wish to thank my respondent, Martina Gnadt, for helpful insights incorporated in the final draft of this paper.

[1] While this optimistic statement cannot cover everyone who claims to be a Christian, I am convinced it represents the views of those who have organized the Neumann Symposium. I assume that it is not necessary to begin warning about prejudices and blinders. This has been done in many places, notably in the following: J. H. Charlesworth, ed., *Jews and Christians. Exploring the Past, Present, and Future*, Shared Ground Among Jews and Christians 1 (New York: Crossroad, 1990); Charlesworth, ed., *Jesus' Jewishness: Exploring the Place of Jesus in Early Judaism*, Shared Ground Among Jews and Christians 2 (New York: American Interfaith Institute and Crossroad, 1991).

[2] E. Schürer, *A History of the Jewish People in the Time of Jesus Christ*, trans. S. Taylor and P. Christie (Edinburgh: T. & T. Clark, 1898), vol. 2, p. 115.

Today we know that any text is misrepresented if we simply remove it from its literary and social context. We recognize how offensive and distorted is the removal of a passage from its context in order to prove some theological idea or system in another context.

The context of all the quotations in this paper is the vibrant, creative world of Early Judaism (250 B.C. to A.D. 200). I wish to salute the steering committee of the Neumann Symposium for not asking me to focus on the Jewish Background of the Lord's Prayer, since that approach, with its preoccupation on Jesus' Prayer, could restrict the amount of light we might receive concerning prayer in Early Judaism. Our vision can therefore encompass the full range of Jewish prayers during the time of Jesus.

In a rudderless society we Christians find a helmsman's direction in the belief that vision, vocation, and vitality come from the conviction that God is present to us today because of the life and teachings of Jesus of Nazareth. His prayers and those of other Jews help sustain us. In disheartening times, it is encouraging to realize that Jesus affirmed that God was Abba, one who always hears the prayers of those who turn to him with a pure heart. In our troubled times, it is enlightening to perceive that Jesus and many other devout Jews of his time looked for the coming of God's rule; they believed that God had not given up on his people but was in the process of fulfilling all his promises through his covenant loyalty.

On target for us now is the recognition that the Jewish apocalyptists, who tended to place God as far from the contaminated earth as conceivable, stressed that angels *united* the divine and human realms. Prayers were heard by God who hears and willingly responds. Note what a Jew wrote in the *Non-Canonical Psalms from Qumran*:[3]

> On the day of [my] d[istress]
> I will call to Yahweh, and my God will answer me.
> *(4Q381 24.7-8)*

Elsewhere in these Dead Sea Scroll psalms we read that the Jew can state that "those who fear you are always before you" (*4Q381 46.6*). As palaeographical evidence shows, this psalm clearly antedates 100 B.C. It was composed by a Palestinian Jew, and it is unwise to understand it only in terms of the Qumran Community (because there is nothing in *4Q381* that indicates composition at Qumran). The need to call on God and the conviction that he "will answer" permeate most sectors of Early Judaism.

[3] For clarification, Josephus' writings and documents in the Apocrypha, Pseudepigrapha, Dead Sea Scrolls, and Rabbinics are placed in italics.

Despite some misinformed publications, the Jews of Jesus' time did not project God out of this world and time. Religious Jews continued to affirm an emphasis of the Davidic Psalms: God is near, attentive, and does hear prayers (Ps. 6:9, 65:2; cf. Prov. 15:29, *Sir.* 4:6). God was near to one who prayed. Many early Jewish prayers, said in numerous settings, ended with the blessing, "Blessed are you, O Lord, who hears prayer" (t.*Ber* 3.7; b.*Ber* 29b).

Observe especially two passages in the *Psalms of Solomon*, written in Jerusalem a few decades prior to the birth of Jesus. In Psalm 6:5 a Jew affirmed that "the Lord has heard the prayers of all who fear God" (*PssSol* 6:5 [Greek]). Later his congregation recited with him in a Jerusalem synagogue the following: "Your ears listen to the hopeful prayer of the poor" (*PssSol* 18:2; cf. also 5:12, 7:7).

As we attempt to appreciate Jewish prayer, it is imperative to comprehend that Jews were convinced that their prayers reached the Creator. Note in particular the pictorial account of how angels scurry to bring before God the prayers of the faithful on earth. The passage is found in *3 Baruch* 11-14 in which Michael, "the holder of the keys of the kingdom of heaven,"[4] descends to "receive the prayers of humans" (*tas deēseis tōn anthrōpōn; 3Bar* 11:4).[5] After hearing a loud voice in heaven commanding the gates to open, Baruch describes what he saw:

> And Michael came. . . . And I saw him holding a very large receptacle, and its depth was that from heaven to earth, and its width that from east to west. And I said, "Lord, what is Michael holding?" And he said to me, "This is where the prayers of men go."
>
> (*3Bar* 11:6-9 [Slavonic]; *OTP*, vol. 1, p. 674)

Michael then takes the receptacle to God.

This vision provides a threefold corrective to some published thoughts about Jewish apocalypticism: Angels do not separate the human and divine worlds; they unite humans with God.[6] Secondly, though conceptually transcendent, God is present liturgically. Thirdly, while removed from the earth that is spinning waywardly, God is attentive and close to those who are near

---

4 All translations from the Pseudepigrapha are according to those in J. H. Charlesworth, ed., *The Old Testament Pseudepigrapha*, 2 vols. (Garden City: Doubleday, 1983, 1985). [*OTP*]

5 The Greek is taken from J.-C. Picard, ed., *Apocalypsis Baruchi Graece*, Pseudepigrapha Veteris Testamenti Graece 2 (Leiden: Brill, 1967).

6 According to a tradition later than *3Bar* an angel "takes all the prayers said in all the synagogues," makes with them a crown, and places it on God's head (*Exodus Rabbah* 21:4).

him by praying to him. Thus *3 Baruch*, written about a generation after the destruction of the Temple, continues through an apocalyptic vision the essential function of the Jerusalem cult. As Michael now completes the cycle of prayer, so before A.D. 70 the spiraling smoke from the sacrifices in the *axis mundi* ascended heavenward to present before God human prayers and petitions.

These preliminary observations on how Jewish prayers united humans with God allow us to begin an exploration of the essence and function of Jewish prayers during the time of Jesus.[7] Fortunately, we can reflect more reliably on the meaning, social function, and essence of Jewish prayer during the time of Jesus[8] because of the publication of form-critical studies on pre-rabbinic prayers,[9] surveys of Jewish prayers in the period from circa 250 B.C. to A.D. 200,[10] recent editions of the prayers preserved among the Dead Sea Scrolls and the Pseudepigrapha, and related studies on early Jewish prayer.[11]

[7] For reliable studies on Jewish prayers by Jewish experts in the field which attempt, at least at times, to be sensitive to the pre-rabbinic phase of Jewish prayers, see B. Martin, *Prayer in Judaism* (New York, London: Basic Books, 1968); J. J. Petuchowski, *Understanding Jewish Prayer* (New York: KTAV, 1972); S. Greenberg, *A Treasury of Thoughts on Jewish Prayer* (Northvale, New Jersey and London: Jason Aronson, 1989); Y. Kirzner, *The Art of Jewish Prayer* (Northvale, New Jersey and London: Jason Aronson, 1991).

Two classic studies must be mentioned: I. Elbogen, *Der jüdische Gottesdienst in seiner geschichtlichen Entwicklung* (Frankfurt am Main: J. Kauffmann Verlag, 1931) and F. C. Grant, "Modern Study of the Jewish Liturgy," *Zeitschrift für die alttestamentliche Wissenschaft* 65 (1953): 59-77.

[8] An informative and popular treatment of daily prayer in Judaism during Jesus' time is J. Jeremias' "Daily Prayer in the Life of Jesus and the Primitive Church," which is found in *The Prayers of Jesus*, Studies in Biblical Theology, Second Series 6 (London: SCM, 1967; Philadelphia: Fortress, 1979), pp. 66-81.

[9] J. Heinemann, *Prayer in the Talmud: Forms and Patterns*, trans. R. S. Sarason, Studia Judaica 9 (Berlin and New York: Walter de Gruyter, 1977). On pp. 302-04 Heinemann provides a "Selected Bibliography" to the most important early secondary literature and rabbinic sources. Also, see J. Heinemann, *La Prière Juive*, trans. J. Dessellier, Les Cahiers de l'Institut Catholique de Lyon 13 (Paris: Société d'Edition Operex, 1984). See the critical assessment of Heinemann's form-critical analysis of rabbinic prayers in L. A. Hoffman, *The Canonization of the Synagogue Service* (Notre Dame, London: University of Notre Dame Press, 1979).

[10] J. H. Charlesworth, "A Prolegomenon to a New Study of the Jewish Background of the Hymns and Prayers in the New Testament," in *Essays in Honour of Yigael Yadin*, ed. G. Vermes and J. Neusner, *Journal of Jewish Studies* 33 (1982) (Oxford: Oxford Centre for Postgraduate Hebrew Studies, 1982), pp. 265-85; Charlesworth, "Jewish Hymns, Odes, and Prayers (ca. 167 B.C.E.-135 C.E.)," in *Early Judaism and its Modern Interpreters*, ed. R. A. Kraft and G. W. E. Nickelsburg, The Bible and its Modern Interpreters (Philadelphia: Fortress; Atlanta: Scholars), pp. 411-36.

[11] See especially D. Flusser, "Psalms, Hymns and Prayers," in *Jewish Writings of the Second Temple Period*, ed. M. E. Stone, Compendia Rerum Iudaicarum ad Novum Testamentum 2.2 (Assen: Van Gorcum; Philadelphia: Fortress, 1984), pp. 551-77. Also see the bibliographical survey by J. Hennig, "Liturgie und das Judentum," *Archiv für Liturgiewissenschaft* 24

The remainder of this study will be focused on the attempt to comprehend six aspects of Jewish prayer.[12] The first three of these clarify the great need for God expressed in Jewish prayers: a dependence on God, an urgency for forgiveness, and finally a desire to converse with God and to know that he is present to hear and respond. Next we shall explore three dimensions of Jewish prayer: it was public and collective, it solidified Israel as a people who prayed, and it was cosmic, both clarifying and uniting times and seasons. In the process we may contemplate the true essence of Jewish prayer, in which spontaneously one can communicate with God directly as one heart speaks silently to another (*cor ad cor loquitur*). Before God speaks, he knows what is in the heart (*Exodus Rabbah* 21:3).

I. Dependence on and Need for God

About the time of Jesus Jews frequently expressed their need for God. Considering themselves "Israel" they repeatedly expressed in public services in the synagogue and the Temple their consciousness of being God's people. In the first petition of the *Amidah* or *Tefillah* (*18 Benedictions*), which surely represents Jewish prayer during the time of Jesus, God is called "our shield and shield of our fathers."[13]

A noteworthy passage is found in the *Psalms of Solomon*:

You are God and we are the people whom you have loved; look and be compassionate, O God of Israel, for we are yours. . . .

(*PssSol* 9:8-9; *OTP*, vol. 2, p. 661)

Beginning decades before the birth of Jesus and probably continuing until the destruction of A.D. 70, this passage was recited in services in Jerusalem by Jews who were close in many ways to the Pharisees.

The story about Daniel was put into written form shortly after the dedication of the Temple by Judas Maccabeus in 164 B.C. (*1Mac* 4), and it was well known and beloved by Jesus' contemporaries. Despite the threats of heathens who could kill him, Daniel prayed three times daily, and he did so boldly and openly before his window as he faced westward towards Jeru-

---

(1982): 113-30. Very important are the articles in H. H. Henrix, ed., *Jüdische Liturgie: Geschichte—Struktur—Wesen*, Quaestiones Disputatae 86 (Freiburg: Herder, 1979).

[12] These categories are only preliminary and somewhat subjective; we need not only surveys and summaries but also—and more importantly—full analyses of the literary and social context of each prayer.

[13] We have no clear evidence of the *Amidah* or *18 Benedictions* before A.D. 70. None of the early Jewish writings cites it. D. Flusser, however, is of the opinion that the *Thanksgiving Hymns* "betrays knowledge of the *Eighteen Benedictions*" ("Psalms, Hymns and Prayers," p. 576).

salem (Dan. 6:10). This story reflects the paradigm that became normative
for all pious Jews; they were to pray three times a day and to face Jerusalem.
Thus, prayer ordered the day and trifurcated it (as we shall see later). According to the Mishnaic tractate *Berakoth* the Shema—Hear, O Israel! The
LORD is our God, the LORD alone[14]—is to be recited twice daily, in the
early morning before sunrise and in the evening at an undetermined time,
perhaps before retiring.

Reading through the *Hodayoth*—the *Thanksgiving Hymns* which were the
"hymnbook" of the group of Jews who left us the Dead Sea Scrolls—provides the impression that the original author, and those who continued his
work by composing other hymns or prayers, lived only for God and were
nourished by blessing him. The ability to open the mouth to utter "the fruit
of the lips" to God was possible only with God's help.

The discovery of hundreds of hymns and prayers composed by the early
Jews and the recovery of collections or hymnbooks like the *Thanksgiving
Hymns*, the *Psalms of Solomon*, the *Non-Canonical Psalms from Qumran*, and
the *Songs of the Sabbath Sacrifice*, leave us with the impression that Jews felt
bound to create new songs or prayers to God. In fact, in the *Psalms of Solomon* we read the exhortation: "Sing a new song to God, who is worthy to
be praised" (*PssSol* 3:1).[15]

The early Jew rejoiced in the revelation of God's will embodied in Torah.
The "Law" was not a burden but a cause of joy and celebration. The Jew
exclaimed, "great is the Law" (m.*Aboth* 6.7). Israelites throughout the land,
especially in synagogues, chanted the 17th Benediction of the *Amidah*, and
exclaimed, "Blessed are you, O Lord, to whom it is good to give thanks."

---

[14] Following the translation of Deut. 6:4 according to *TANAKH: A New Translation of the
Holy Scriptures According to the Traditional Hebrew Text* (Philadelphia: Jewish Publication
Society, 1985). Note the interpretation of the Shema in the Jewish work masquerading as
instruction by Orpheus (prior to 70 B.C.) to his son and pupil Musaeus:

There is an ancient saying about him:
"he is one"—self-completing, and all things completed by him.
(*Ps-Orph* 9-10 [Long Version]; *OTP*, vol. 2, p. 799)

The Jewish author was interpreting Deut. 6:4.

Deut. 6:4 can be translated in more than one way. It can be rendered "Hear, O Israel!
The LORD our God, the LORD is one." In a Jewish pseudepigraphon dating from the late
Hellenistic or early Roman period we find an endorsement of the latter interpretation of
Deut. 6:4,

God is one, one in very truth.

(*FrgsPoetWrks* [Sophocles]; *OTP*, vol. 2, p. 825)

[15] Of course the same refrain is found in the Davidic Psalms; but, it is important to note
that Jews long after the completion of the 150 Davidic Psalms felt compelled to compose new
hymns, prayers, and psalms. In fact, the number of psalms in the Psalter increased to 155.

The authors of the *Thanksgiving Hymns* at Qumran repeatedly chanted praise to God for Torah (viz. *1QH* 10.31-33). Like the psalmists who composed and compiled the Davidic Psalter,[16] the Jew hungered for God. Throughout the day and night Jews could be found devotedly praying to God (cf. *1QH* 10.20).

The need for God is abundantly evident in the early Jewish prayers, hymns, and psalms. The devout Jew in the land and during the time of Hillel and Jesus would urge us to comprehend that to live is to pray.

II. Need for Acceptance, Forgiveness, and Justification

The need for God was expressed above all as Jews depended solely on God for acceptance, forgiveness, and justification. Since this is the dominant element in early Jewish prayer, and since it continues to be overlooked it will occupy much of our discussion. It is obviously imperative to perceive the Jewish perspective: faithful obedience to the Law and continuous ritual cleansings and sacrifices did not earn salvation or forgiveness.

Jews readily admitted they were sinful and incapable of fulfilling Torah, God's will. The devout Jew who composed the *Prayer of Manasseh*, probably sometime before the public ministry of Jesus in a context unknown to us today, felt his own unworthiness and deep sinfulness. Affirming that God had "appointed grace for me, (I) who am a sinner" (v. 8), the author voices these penetrating lines of poetry:

> And now behold I am bending
> the knees of my heart before you;
> and I am beseeching your kindness.
> I have sinned, O Lord, I have sinned;
> and I certainly know my sins.
> I beseech you;
> forgive me, O Lord, forgive me!
> (*PrMan* vv. 11-13; *OTP*, vol. 2, p. 634)

He continues by affirming that the "God of our fathers" is the "God of those who repent" and that "in me you will manifest all your grace."

A "Prayer of Manasseh," which is not to be confused with the *Prayer of Manasseh*, has been found among the *Non-Canonical Psalms from Qumran*. In it we find the following expression of sin and need for God's forgiveness:

---

[16] See especially Ps. 61:1, 69:13, 84:8, and 102:1. Also note *3Mac* 1:24, according to which the "crowd" was engaged in prayer.

I wait for Your saving presence,
and I cringe before You *because of my s[in]s.*
For [*You*] have magnified [*Your mercies*]
But I have multiplied guilt.

(*4Q381* 33.9)[17]

This prayer indicates the need for forgiveness among early Jews besides those within the Qumran Community; there are reasons to think that it may not have been composed at Qumran. Running through early Jewish prayers is a repetitive refrain of unworthiness. *Psalm 155* in an early Davidic Psalter contains the affirmation that "no one living is righteous before you" (*11QPs^a* 155. 8).

This admission of unrighteousness, despite what most publications imply and Christians assume, also pertains to the most revered and righteous person in Early Judaism, specifically the High Priest. The popular depictions of him as arrogant and self-righteous are due to a failure to realize the redactional and polemical nature of the New Testament portrayals of the high priest.

Though written about 130 years after the time when the high priest officiated over the Temple services, the Mishnaic tractate *Yoma* records a tradition that is reliable in its general depiction; but it is difficult to date and assess how accurate is its reconstruction. The high priest knew and confessed publicly in the Temple on the Day of Atonement his sinfulness. Putting his hands on the bullock which he would sacrifice for his sins, the high priest made a confession:

O God, I have committed iniquity, transgressed,
and sinned before thee, I and my house.
O God, forgive the iniquities and transgressions
and sins which I have committed and transgressed
and sinned before thee, I and my house.

(m.*Yoma* 3.8)[18]

While we should not take these words as *ipsissima verba* of the high priest, it is important to observe that around A.D. 200, in Rabbi Judah's Rabbinic Academy in which the Mishnah was completed, Rabbis claimed that the high priest, highly revered and honored, was acknowledged to be one who

[17] E. M. Schuller, *Non-Canonical Psalms from Qumran: A Pseudepigraphic Collection*, Harvard Semitic Studies 28 (Atlanta: Scholars, 1986), p. 151.
[18] Translated by H. Danby in *The Mishnah* (Oxford: Oxford University Press, 1933), p. 165. I have supplied the poetic divisions.

had sinned and needed to express publicly his sins and to sacrifice to God for them, humbly requesting forgiveness.

This historical reconstruction, based on rabbinic sources, is at least partly anchored for pre-70 Judaism by the *Temple Scroll*'s account[19] of the high priest's sacrifice of a bullock for his own sins on the Day of Atonement (*11QTemple* 5.15-16.e). It is also highly probable that something resembling the words recorded in the Mishnah (*Yoma*) were actually spoken before A.D. 70 in the Temple by the high priest.

According to tractate *Yoma* the high priest confessed his guilt a second time. Laying his two hands upon the bullock he said,

> O God, I have committed iniquity and transgressed
>   and sinned before thee,
> I and my house and the children of Aaron,
>   thy holy people.
> O God, forgive, I pray, the iniquities
>   and transgressions and sins which I have committed
>   and transgressed and sinned before thee,
> I and my house and the children of Aaron,
>   thy holy people.
>
> (m.*Yoma* 4.2)[20]

After slaughtering the bullock and continuing with the ceremony on the Day of Atonement, the high priest can now confess the sins of the nation:

> O God, thy people, the House of Israel,
>   have committed iniquity, transgressed,
>   and sinned before thee.
> O God, forgive, I pray, the iniquities
>   and transgressions and sins
>   which thy people, the House of Israel,
>   have committed and transgressed
>   and sinned before thee.
>
> (m.*Yoma* 6.2)[21]

The final word of this confession included the name Yahweh as it was written and not according to the perpetual *qere* "Adonai, Lord." On hearing this

---

[19] The *Temple Scroll* probably reached its present edited form in the early decades of the first century B.C. See M. Hengel, J. H. Charlesworth, and D. Mendels, "The Polemical Character of 'On Kingship' in the Temple Scroll: An Attempt at Dating 11QTemple," *Journal of Jewish Studies* 37 (1986): 28-38.

[20] Translation by Danby; arrangement by me.

[21] Translation by Danby; arrangement by me.

name—ineffable elsewhere and expressible only by the high priest in the Temple—the priests and the people in the Temple court knelt and bowed, saying, "Blessed be the name of the glory of his kingdom for ever and ever" (m.*Yoma* 6.2).[22] Despite the shaping and altering of traditions from A.D. 70 to 200, it is clear that during the Day of Atonement Israel, collectively and publicly, following the example of the spiritual leader, the high priest, confessed sin and unworthiness, and appealed to God for forgiveness and acceptance. Forgiveness was desperately sought; and it could not be obtained by obeying the Torah or offering sacrifices. It could be obtained from God alone and only through his grace.

The Qumranites knew that "no one is righteous before" God (*1QH* 16.11). Note, in particular, the following passage: "I shall wait (with assurance) for your forgiveness" (*1QH* 10.21-22). The Qumran Covenanters probably chanted these affirmations collectively in the recognition that "righteousness (does not belong) to the human (*'ᵉnôsh*)" (*1QH* 4.30), because "all the works of righteousness (belong only) to the Most High God" (*1QH* 4.31).

The hymn (or prayer) in the last column of the *Rule of the Community* (the major book of rules for the Qumran Community) affirms humanity's unworthiness and reliance upon God alone for forgiveness and acceptance:

> For I (know) to God (belongs) my justification,[23]
> and in his hand (is) the perfection of my way,
> along with the uprightness of my heart;
> and by his righteousness my evils are blotted out.[24]
>
> (*1QS* 11.2-3)

> For is to man (the decision regarding) his way?
> And surely the human (*'ᵉnôsh*) cannot establish his
>   step;
> for to God (is) justification,
> and from his hand (comes) perfection of the way.
>
> (*1QS* 11.10-11)

Human justification is due to God's grace alone, because no one can be or is righteous before God (*1QH* 16.11). Fortunately God's grace is abun-

---

[22] Danby's translation.

[23] In Qumran Hebrew *mishpāṭ* means more than "judgment," which is its essential meaning in Biblical Hebrew. It denotes frequently God's eschatological decision on behalf of a human being. God judges (*shpṭ*) humans not according to what they deserve but according to his covenant loyalty and grace.

[24] Presumably "blotted out" from the book of life in which records are kept (cf. esp. *ApAb*).

dant (*1QH* 10.14). This emphasis is not unique to the Dead Sea Scrolls; it is also found, for example, in the expansion to the Davidic Psalter (*Ps 153:6*) and the *Prayer of Manasseh* (v. 8).

Perhaps a question arises at this point: Was not Paul the genius who created the concept that salvation derives solely from God's grace? The answer is "no." Long before Paul, the Qumran covenanters affirmed that salvation is by God's grace alone;[25] forgiveness is only through God. Despite a still lingering misunderstanding about early Jewish theology, there is no Jewish text that conveys the claim that obedience to Torah can save the pious and faithful one.

What then was Paul's contribution? Paul inherited from many sectors of Early Judaism the pre-Christian Jewish insight that salvation is solely through God's grace, but he stressed this thought and made it central. He inherited from Jesus' followers the claim that Jesus died as the Messiah, emphasizing that the crucifixion and resurrection had effectively provided full forgiveness and acceptance for all who were faithful. He inherited from his Jewish teachers and Jesus' followers the concept of faith; but he emphasized the absolute necessity of believing that God through Jesus Christ had redeemed *all* humanity.[26] Finally, Paul added the notion that freedom and hope come with *faith* in Christ's crucifixion as the means of obtaining God's gracious forgiveness instead of deserved condemnation.[27] In developing these insights Paul, who was born a Pharisee, remained thoroughly a first-century Jew; he was shaped by his social and intellectual environment.

As we have seen confessions of unworthiness and need for God's forgiveness permeate Early Judaism. In synagogues throughout the land and in homes each day the sixth benediction in the *Amidah* was recited:

> Forgive us, our Father, for we have sinned against thee.
> Erase and blot out our transgressions
>   from before thine eyes.

[25] Of course, the definition of "grace" is not assumed to be identical in the Dead Sea Scrolls and in Paul's letters. It is also not obvious that "grace" consistently has the same meaning within each corpus.

[26] I am still uncertain what Paul meant in Romans 11:1-2 ("I ask, then, has God rejected his people? Heavens no. . . . God has not rejected his people whom he foreknew."). Do these words indicate that Paul affirmed "two covenants"? See the papers from the 1989 Neumann Symposium in *The Church and Israel: Romans 9-11*, ed. D. L. Migliore, *The Princeton Seminary Bulletin*, Supplementary Issue, no. 1 (Princeton, 1990).

[27] For a detailed discussion of Paul's theology in light of Qumran theologies see J. Murphy-O'Connor and J. H. Charlesworth, eds., *Paul and the Dead Sea Scrolls*, Christian Origins Library (New York: Crossroad, 1990). Paul inherited from some sectors of Judaism a critique of "the Law," but he added (somewhat inconsistently) a denigration of "Law," but not Torah.

For thou art abundantly compassionate.

Blessed art thou, O Lord, who forgives readily.[28]

The early Jew was assured of speedy forgiveness; sins were not borne as an eternal curse. The Jewish system for forgiveness and acceptance by God— and only he mattered to the religious Jew—was efficient and efficacious; and it was not delimited to the Temple. The Jew rejoiced daily in saying "your mercy, O Lord, upholds us" (17th Benediction of the *Amidah*). Today, within Judaism and Christianity the institutional means for obtaining and experiencing God's acceptance are apparently less efficient for most members of God's covenant people than in the time of Jesus.[29]

III. NEED TO CONVERSE WITH GOD SPONTANEOUSLY

The Jew felt the need to converse with God and to do so spontaneously.[30] Sometimes this conversation was through silence and in meditation. The Mishnah provides ample evidence that the Shema, which was to be recited at least twice daily, could be said, at times, without speaking out loud: "If a man recited the *Shema* but not loudly enough for himself to hear, he has fulfilled his obligation" (m.*Ber* 2.3). The Jew believed that God could hear the voice of the heart. When he lacked the proper words by which to pray, King David is reputed to have asked God to "understand what is in my heart" (*Midrash Tehillim* 5.6).

Although the century before A.D. 70 saw the creation of statutory prayers like the *Amidah* or *18 Benedictions* which were to be recited daily (m.*Ber* 4.3), stress was placed on the need to be spontaneous and personal in praying. Rabbi Simeon exhorted that "when you pray do not make your prayer a fixed form" (m.*Aboth* 2.13). Rabbi Eliezer also warned against depending on set prayers: "He that makes his prayer a fixed task, his prayer is no supplication" (m.*Ber* 4.4). During Jesus' time many religious leaders exhorted Jews to offer *personal* prayers and to struggle for appropriate words. Probably Paul was reflecting this ethos when two decades before the destruction of 70 he wrote these words on prayer:

Likewise the Spirit helps us in our weakness;

for we do not know how to pray as we ought,

---

[28] Translation by Heinemann in *Prayer in the Talmud*, p. 27.

[29] See R.K. Fenn, *The Secularization of Sin* (Louisville: Westminster/John Knox, 1991).

[30] See Kirzner's "The Historical Background of the Need to Communicate with God," in *The Art of Jewish Prayer*, pp. 6-7.

> but the Spirit itself[31] intercedes for us with
> ineffable sighs.[32] And the one who fathoms the hearts
> knows what is the mind of the Spirit, because the Spirit
> intercedes for the holy ones according to God.
>
> (Rom. 8:26-27)

The early Jews knew how difficult it is to put into words an appropriate and representative prayer; before God one becomes speechless. Experiencing how difficult it is to discern what is in our own deepest thoughts and feelings, it is unnerving to comprehend that God fathoms even deeper into our innermost being. Fortunately, the Jew also experienced the assistance of angels and the spirit of God (and for some the Holy Spirit).[33] The Jerusalem Talmud (5th cent. A.D.) records the tradition, which must be ancient, that God hears the faintest whisper (y.*Ber* 9.1). Here we meet the essence of Jewish prayer: spontaneous communication with the Creator as *cor ad cor loquitur*.[34]

Jesus' Prayer, the Lord's Prayer, was a model for such personal and spontaneous prayers.[35] Like other personal prayers it is brief, couched in a simple style, and addresses God in the second person. It was the outline to be used when praying spontaneously. That the Lord's Prayer is a model is reflected in Matthew's *houtōs oun proseuchesthe hymeis*, "you are to pray like this ..." (Mt. 6:9). For Jesus, then, personal and spontaneous prayer should follow this outline: praise to Abba, plea for a world-wide recognition of his holiness, appeal for the coming of his rule or kingdom on earth, petition for daily sustenance and forgiveness of sins, and request for guidance from unbearable temptation.[36] Later, when the Jewish model for personal and spontaneous prayer was forgotten, the Lord's Prayer developed into a statutory prayer with a full ending.

[31] As is well known, "spirit" in Greek is neuter grammatically and the pronoun in Rom. 8:26 is *auto*. Some translations have "himself" here; I have attempted to avoid sexist language but am not implying that the spirit is an "it."

[32] The Greek *stenagmois alalētois* of Rom. 8:26 denotes more than "inexpressible" sighs (as in the Vulgate's *inenarrabilis*); it denotes sights too deep, precious, or conceptually pure (or complex) to pour forth into speech.

[33] See my introductory chapter to *Jesus and the Dead Sea Scrolls* (Doubleday, in press).

[34] As P. Lenhardt states, "La prière, admirablement désignée comme 'le service (Abodah) du coeur' est un des piliers de la Torah orale." See his preface in *La Prière Juive*, p. 8.

[35] See Heinemann, *Prayer in the Talmud*, p. 191.

[36] I am convinced that Jesus taught this prayer in Aramaic. The Old Syriac, and probably the original Aramaic, mean "do not allow us to enter into temptation." See J. H. Charlesworth, "The *Beth Essentiae* and the Permissive Meaning of the Hiphil (Aphel)," in *Of Scribes and Scrolls* [Strugnell Festschrift], ed. H. W. Attridge, J. J. Collins, and T. H. Tobin, College Theology Society Resources in Religion 5 (New York and London: Lanham, 1991), pp. 67-78; esp. p. 78.

The Greek magical papyri contain prayers that try to control and manipulate God; note the following prayer:

> Hither, come hither, hither come; respond
> With prophecies, give presage in night's hour.[37]

Jewish prayers do not attempt to control God. Personal prayer was to ask for God's control and will. Jesus' teachings and prayer emphasized obedience to God's will; he urged us to pray "your will be done on earth as it is in heaven."

IV. Jewish Prayers Were Public and Collective

Jewish prayers were not only intensely personal and private; they were also part of the great institution in Early Judaism. The house of prayer was the Temple; Jesus as other Jews of his time referred to the Temple as the "house of prayer" (Mk. 11:17). In it God was held to be present.[38] To it, especially during high moments like the time of circumcision and Bar Mitzwah, and during the great festival pilgrimages, came Jews from Parthia to the east, Egypt to the south, Rome and Greece to the west, and Syria to the north. Here in the Temple could be found choirs of Levites singing, often accompanied with harp, cymbal, and even trumpet.[39] Here the hymnbook of the Second Temple, the Davidic Psalms, could be heard not only when read in study groups but also in chants accompanied by music.

The grandeur of the Temple was greater than we imagined a decade ago.[40] A stone in the lower course of the western retaining wall weighs over 400 tons. This and related discoveries help confirm Josephus' descriptions of the Temple (*Ant* 5.224; 15.392) and the amazement of Jesus' disciples: "Look, Teacher, what magnificent stones, and what magnificent buildings" (Mk. 13:1). The gold, brass, and silver shone in the day from the blazing sun and sparkled in the night from gigantic torches; the Temple was alive with intricate colors, especially to one praying on the hill to the east, in the Garden of Gethsemane.

All human senses were aroused in the Temple. The smell of the burning

[37] H. D. Betz, ed., *The Greek Magical Papyri in Translation* (Chicago, London: University of Chicago Press, 1986), vol. 1, p. 111.

[38] See especially the *Temple Scroll* 45:14, 46:12, 51:7-8.

[39] For a reliable description of worship in the Temple see "Priesthood and Temple Worship," in E. Schürer, *The History of the Jewish People in the Age of Jesus Christ (175 B.C.-A.D. 135)*, rev. and ed. G. Vermes, et al. (Edinburgh: T. & T. Clark, 1979), vol. 2, pp. 237-308.

[40] See J. H. Charlesworth, "The Jesus of History and the Archaeology of Palestine," in *Jesus Within Judaism*, Anchor Bible Reference Library 1 (New York: Doubleday, 1988), pp. 103-30; esp. pp. 118-20.

incense was intoxicating. The cavalcade of sounds was overwhelming: the melodious tones of Levites singing, the blast of trumpet and shofar, the chanting of priests (sometimes numbering into the thousands), the cries of animals about to be sacrificed, and the humming voices of prayers being offered and of sacred texts being read aloud. The eye was mesmerized by the flashing rays from gold and other precious metals and jewels as they reflected the glare of sun or fires, by the movement of full white and multicolored priestly garments, by the ascending trails of smoke from sacrificial fires, by the rows of priests with bowls of sacrificial blood, and by the majestic size of the Temple mount, the porticoes, esplanades, and the Temple itself with its massive and intricate doors. Allowing for the presupposition of the necessity of animal sacrifices, which is foreign to us today, it is easy to imagine how in the Temple one could experience the presence of God and the possibility of communicating directly with him. Only from a distance can we be empathetic with Jesus and other Jews who stood in the Temple and heard chanted or recited themselves the words of Psalm 26:8:

> O Lord, I love the abode of your Temple,[41]
>   the dwelling-place of your glory.

How moving must have been the poetry of Psalm 84:

> How lovely is your dwelling-place,
>   O Lord of hosts.
> My soul longs, indeed yearns for the courts of the Lord;
>   my heart and flesh shout for joy to the living God.
>   (Ps. 84:2-3 [following the vss. in Heb.])

Elsewhere in Jerusalem in numerous places Jews gathered in a synagogue and in a *Bêt Midrāsh* (a House of Study) to discuss their own interpretations of Torah, both written and oral, and they united together in prayers said by Jews elsewhere and in prayers special to their own group.

V. PRAYER SOLIDIFIED ISRAEL

Prayer solidified Israel as a people galvanized with God. Collective and private prayers were said in more places than in the Temple, a synagogue, and in a *Bêt Midrāsh*.

In the home, meals were sacred. Prayers are known to be given after and sometimes before the meal (perhaps in some settings before and after the

---

[41] The Hebrew is literally, "your house"; "house" denotes "Temple."

meal). This custom clearly antedates Jesus' time and his family and associates were accustomed to it; they probably followed the tradition.

The tradition was ancient. In the second-century B.C. book of *Jubilees*, the account of Abraham's death involves a feast in which he eats a meal and then blesses God (*Jub* 22:4-6; *OTP*, vol. 2, p. 97). In a book that antedates Jesus and his time, namely the *Letter of Aristeas*,[42] a prayer is offered before a great feast in Alexandria. During Jesus' time a prayer after the meal was said in a form similar to the Grace After Meals:

> Blessed art thou, Lord our God, King of the universe, who sustainest the whole world with goodness, kindness and mercy. Thou givest food to all creatures, for thy mercy endures forever.[43]

Before eating the bread the following well-known prayer may have been said in the first century A.D., in a form somewhat similar to that said today:

> Blessed art thou, Lord our God, King of the universe, who bringest forth bread from the earth.[44]

There is some evidence, not easy to assess and comprehend, that special meals were frequently arranged. These *Ḥaburah* meals were for invited guests of a specified number. There were cautions about Jews with whom one should not enjoy a meal and grace (cf. b.*Ber* 43b; b.*San* 23a). At the conclusion of the meal grace was to be recited, probably by a leader.

In the *Bêt Midrāsh* prayers were recited before and after the reading and studying of scripture and the preaching based on Torah. According to a form-critical study of Jewish prayers, the *Bêt Midrāsh* prayers never mention the Tetragrammaton (Yahweh) but frequently use the "he"-style of address to God and refer to him as "King" and "Holy One."[45]

One of the most important of the *Bêt Midrāsh* prayers is the popular *ʿalênû lᵉshabbeaḥ*:

> It is our duty to praise the Master of all,
> to exalt the Creator of the universe,
> who has not made us like the nations of the world
> and has not placed us like the families of the earth;

[42] *LetAris*, lines 184-86 (*OTP*, vol. 2, p. 25).
[43] For the Hebrew and English, see P. Birnbaum, *Daily Prayer Book* (New York: Hebrew Publishing Co., 1949, 1977), pp. 759-60.
[44] Birnbaum, *Daily Prayer Book*, pp. 773-74.
[45] See Heinemann, *Prayer in the Talmud*, p. 270.

who has not designed our destiny to be like theirs,
nor our lot like that of all their multitude.[46]

This form is recited today in synagogues throughout the world, and is a later edited form of the prayer said prior to 70. Such prayers unite Jews.

Along with other pre-70 Jews, Jesus urged his followers to offer personal prayers which embodied the collective nature of prayer. He said to pray "give *us* this day *our* daily bread, and forgive *us* our debts as *we* forgive *our* debtors, and do not allow *us* to be tempted, but deliver *us* from temptation."

VI. Prayer was Cosmic and Calendrical

To study early Jewish prayer is to become involved in the daily lives of the Jews. Prayer was not an accessory; it was the fabric of existence. The day was ordered according to the times of prayer. Especially in Jerusalem was this evident; as is well known Peter and John go up to the Temple "at the hour of prayer" (Acts 3:1), that is at 3 p.m. when sacrifices along with prayers were being offered in the Temple (Ex. 29:39, Lev. 6:20; also see Josephus' *Ant* 14). The year was ordered by prayers; each year began with the religious festival of Rosh Ha-Shana and the most important day of the year, the Day of Atonement or Yom Kippur, which (as we have seen) was an honored day when every devout Jew, from the high priest to the lowest 'am haaretz', after ritual purification, prayers of contrition, and sacrifice, felt accepted by the most intimate One. Prayer was not only a means of experiencing oneness with oneself and solidarity with Israel (past, present, and future); it was the vehicle by which the devout Jew became united again, after Adam and Eve's trespass, with the cosmos and especially with the Creator.

The different calendars known in Early Judaism, especially in the second century B.C.,[47] caused major problems for liturgy, prayer, and the observance of Sabbath and festivals. As one of the Dead Sea Scrolls states, the Jew knew that God "will set for me times" (4Q381.2). Not only was it imperative to observe Sabbath on the proper day—and not, for example, on

---

[46] See Birnbaum, *Daily Prayer Book*, pp. 135-36. See also Heinemann's comments on the antiquity of this prayer in *Prayer in the Talmud*, p. 3.

[47] More than two calendars are now known: the lunar calendar of the Temple cultus and established Judaism, and the numerous solar calendars known according to 1 Enoch, Jubilees, and many of the Dead Sea Scrolls. See especially, S. Talmon, *King, Cult and Calendar in Ancient Israel: Collected Essays* (Jerusalem: Magnes, 1986); S. Talmon, *The World of Qumran from Within: Collected Studies* (Jerusalem: Magnes; Leiden: Brill, 1989). Talmon has shown me the Qumranic calendrical text given him to publish by J. T. Milik; it is obvious that many Jews in the centuries before the destruction of 70 were struggling with calendrical issues.

Tuesday—but prayer and worship on earth must be in harmony and in sequence with the angels in heaven who followed the celestial liturgy according to the time ordained by God at creation.[48]

Prayer in Judaism was cosmic. It clarified and unified times, seasons, years, and jubilees. The author of the *Wisdom of Solomon* urged the Israelite to rise before the sun and to "pray at the dawning of light" (*Wis.* 16:28), and the Davidic Psalter indicates that from ancient times the faithful covenanter rose in the early morning to pray (Ps. 88:13). The *Rule of the Community* specified praying at the beginning of the day and the night (*1QS* 11.10; cf. *1QH* 4.6). The Dead Sea Scrolls preserve the morning and evening prayers said by the Qumran covenanters, according to which, as "sons of light," they participated in the cosmic appearance of light in the morning and the onslaught of darkness at night (*4Q503-504*).[49] The twilight period in the morning before the appearance of the sun, and the twilight moments in the evening after the setting of the sun but before the coming of darkness were sacred times in which to pray. The worshiper participated in the ordering of the cosmos and the cosmic struggle between light and darkness (cf. *1QM*).

At Qumran the biblical notion that the human on earth praised God as do the angels in heaven received a novel development: the human was joined on earth by angels in celebrating God.[50] This worship occurred in the Qumran Community on earth, which was, as it were, an antechamber of heaven.

VII. Summary

The study of Jewish prayer provides us with a picture of pre-70 Judaism in the Land that contrasts markedly with the chaotic situation imagined from studying Josephus and some of the apocryphal books. Worship, especially the daily prayers, notably the Shema and Amidah, provided a heart and essence to Judaism that in one religious dimension protected Judaism both from a priestly centripetal dominance and from chaotically centrifugal groups.

Although our work should be seen as prolegomenon to a full and detailed study of the text and context of each Jewish prayer, we may conclude that

[48] See especially *1QS* 11.7-10; *1QH* 1.7-20, 4.6; cf. 4.23; *Amidah* (the 18th Benediction), *PssSol* 18:10-12.

[49] See M. Baillet, *Qumrân Grotte 4: III (4Q482-4Q520)*, Discoveries in the Judaean Desert 7 (Oxford: Clarendon Press, 1982).

[50] See the judicious comments by M. Weinfeld, "The Heavenly Praise in Unison," in *Meqor Hajjim: Festschrift für Georg Molin zum 75. Geburtstag*, ed. I. Seybold (Graz: Akademische Durck- u. Verlagsanstalt, 1983), pp. 427-37; esp. p. 429.

early Jewish prayers demonstrate three human needs: a dependence on God, a thirst for acceptance, forgiveness, and justification, and a hunger to converse with God. The three most significant dimensions of Jewish prayers were their collective and public nature, the means by which they solidified Israel as God's people, and the cosmic and calendric harmony they brought to human existence. The essence of Jewish prayer runs throughout each of these needs and dimensions; it witnessed direct communication with God, which can transcend oral communication as *cor ad cor loquitur*. As J. Jeremias stressed, *"Jesus came from a people who knew how to pray"* [italics his].[51]

Jewish authorities today lament that "Jews don't know how to pray," that "they don't know how to talk to God in prayer." The reason given is that "Jews are not sure what they believe about God: Does He exist: Does He hear and answer prayer?"[52]

Rather than an occasion for celebrating Christians' superiority over Jews, these words should arrest us. They should help us heed the advice of many Christian leaders who warn us that we have lost the art of prayer.[53] Surely one way back to authentic praying, conversation with the Beloved-Incredible-One, is through an appreciation of Jewish prayer during Jesus' time.

We have heard the convictions of devout Jews roughly contemporaneous with Jesus; they claimed to have experienced the presence of the living God. We read in hundreds of documents that date in or near the first century A.D. the claim that Jews *knew* God heard and answered their prayers. Such Jews would state unequivocally that *God was experienced*, and that they conversed with him through words, both collectively and privately, and in silence (*cor ad cor loquitur*).

These observations and insights provide a cornucopia of fruits sought for by the founders of the Neumann Symposium: if Christians today would share the early religious Jews' experience, then we would not be so far away from the realization of a monumental dream preserved in an unusually important Jewish prayer: "thy kingdom come, thy will be done on earth as it

[51] Jeremias, *The Prayers of Jesus*, p. 66.

[52] H. S. Kushner, "Foreword," in *A Treasury of Thoughts on Jewish Prayer*, ed. S. Greenberg (Northvale, New Jersey: Jason Aronson, 1989), p. xi.

[53] These books are too well known and numerous to need citing. S. J. Grenz urges us Christians to become a praying community. His model is the worship of the earliest Christians, which is in harmony with our method and in line with the Jewish traditions we have cited. See Grenz, *Prayer: The Cry for the Kingdom* (Peabody, Massachusetts, 1988). Would that more Christians and Jews comprehended that the insight that "true praying is a learned art, requiring understanding in order to be developed. . . . True communication with God is learned, the result of both intellectual reflection and personal diligence" (p. 6).

is in heaven."[54] And we would more perceptively sing George Herbert's insightful thought:

> Come, my Joy, my Love, my Heart:
> Such a Joy, as none can move:
> Such a Love, as none can part:
> Such a Heart, as joys in love.[55]

[54] Following the sermon in early synagogal services (but perhaps postdating the first century) the congregation prayed for the coming of the kingdom of heaven; the Qaddish originally ended with words such as "may he establish his kingdom" in our day.

[55] This prayer and other marvelous compositions, including Jewish prayers, are collected in G. Appleton, *The Oxford Book of Prayer* (Oxford and New York: Oxford University Press, 1990 [reprint of 1985 edition]). The quotation is from p. 7. I have concluded with Herbert's prayerful hymn because our academic year here at Princeton Theological Seminary ends with a commencement in Princeton University Chapel, with the stir of kettle drums, the melodious peal of trumpets, and the collective singing of these words.

The Lord's Prayer in the Gospels of Matthew and Luke

by Donald Juel

I. Introduction

Few who have followed the publication of biblical studies over the last two decades would disagree that a revolution of sorts is in progress. Confidence that historical study will provide a secure foundation on which to erect interpretations has been undermined to the degree that some are willing to abandon it altogether. And if establishing "the facts" seems less feasible and less promising, the acids of criticism have also eroded faith in the old Romantic hermeneutic, familiar to students of Christian tradition, according to which the goal of interpretation is conversation with the "genius" of another human being, whether that be the evangelist, the anonymous storyteller in early Christian circles, or Jesus himself. Unfamiliar terms like "deep structures" and "narrative world" have become more common. I am not surprised that in view of all the possibilities and uncertainties, some young interpreters are paralyzed.

Scholarship need not be paralyzing, but there are clear challenges to be met. The present situation requires modesty among Bible readers. Public conversation about the scriptures will continue to be a stumbling block for those who cannot resist the temptation to be like God, knowing good and evil. Insisting that the Bible is the fundament on which we ground our theology and our views of life has a hollow ring when interpreters can find no way to agree on what the Bible means. We have only the Bible as it lives within the community of interpreters; interpretations can be sustained only to the degree that they can convince others, which in turn presumes a conversation in which reasons can be offered for believing one thing or another. Scriptural authority thus depends upon the sorts of interpretive conversations generated. We have the church's testimony that the scriptures have a word for us and that where two or three are gathered in Jesus' name to study God's word the Spirit is present and at work. Our task is to trust those promises and to learn how to work together so that study can enrich and enliven our imaginations for a more fruitful hearing of God's word.

The unsettled state of the interpretive enterprise requires at least a few words about what a study of the Lord's Prayer should involve. I presume that this conference is being held because we have reason to expect that the Lord's Prayer will continue to serve as a vehicle for our conversation with God. I take it as significant that my assigned topic is "The Lord's Prayer in the Gospels of Matthew and Luke." That is somewhat different from "The Lord's Prayer in the Mouth of Jesus," or "The Lord's Prayer in Q." It is even different from "Matthew's Understanding of the Lord's Prayer." While study of possible Aramaic precursors of the Greek versions of the Lord's Prayer is legitimate and even interesting, and while reconstructing the history of tradition is not without significance for reading the Gospels, my assignment is to interpret the Prayer within its Gospel settings. And the narratives cannot be collapsed into the intentions of some historical writers, even if those writers and their intentions could be known. The Gospel narratives themselves are primary.

There are some important implications for the language we use in our interpretive conversations. We should be suspicious of words like "secondary" or "later," noting how easily they are exchanged for "inauthentic." Few interpreters would deny that the Lord's Prayer in substantial form derives from Jesus of Nazareth. It is likewise clear that the prayer we know as "the Lord's Prayer" owes its present form not simply to translation but also to expansion that occurred within Christian circles. What ought to be of primary interest to us is the scriptural form(s) of the Lord's Prayer, not a reconstructed Aramaic "original." The setting within which the Prayer is heard should be the scriptural settings, not the ministry of the historical Jesus (even if that could be known with some certainty). The scriptures are the "norming norm" for our talk about God and our conversation with God. Because the scriptures are perhaps the one thing we have in common within the Christian family, they have the most promise of shaping and directing our mutual conversation.

The question is how the scriptures will be heard—or in this case, how the Lord's Prayer will be heard in its scriptural settings. It is of considerable significance that we know something about the larger scriptural setting—and the scriptures' own setting in the Greek-speaking Jewish world of the first century. That is true first because the language is not our own. It has a long and noble history within Christian tradition, which will itself condition our hearing and praying of the Prayer, but the Greek is not our tongue, and even the English words used to render it ("kingdom," "Father," "heaven") are foreign enough—and sufficiently offensive to some—to require some reflection. To say that our hearing and praying of the Lord's Prayer will take its cue from the scriptures is not to settle the matter of interpretation but to locate it.

How shall we hear the Lord's Prayer—and how shall we pray it? Hearing is a function of our own experience as well as of the study of others. Some things will strike us as interesting that others have taken for granted. It is difficult to imagine a study of the Prayer that does not take seriously the challenge offered by many within the Christian family who cannot speak the opening words, "Our Father," without some intense experience of alienation. It is not only women who may have difficulty speaking the words; there are men who have no sense that there is a "Father" behind the dim unknown keeping watch above his own, and there are many who have no sense of the "we" presupposed by the Prayer. Language that earlier generations might have taken for granted may now require attention if the Prayer is to serve as a vehicle for conversation with God.

My exegetical study takes cues both from the scriptural context within which the Prayer is to be heard and from my reading of the experience of Christians for whom the interpreting is done. I presume that all of the studies will contribute to a fresh hearing of the Prayer that will open our imaginations to a richer conversation with God.

II. The "Our Father"

One of the issues that cannot be avoided in our present setting is the opening of the Prayer, which in Roman Catholic piety serves as an identification of the Prayer itself, the "Our Father." How shall we pray those words? It is surely not insignificant that a portion of the Christian family finds the language alienating, if not downright offensive. The reality is that praying the Prayer separates out many of "us" who are invited to speak to God as "Father." The Prayer does not facilitate conversation with God but blocks it; it does not build a community but pulls it apart.

To some degree that may be inevitable. The sword that is God's word has a double edge. That God is as intimately related to us as a parent may be experienced as a threat. That God has "searched me and known me," that there is no place where I am cut off from God's presence (Ps. 139) is disquieting if I have something to conceal.

There are ways in which the word of God ought not be an offense, however. There are ways in which one can be alienated with no hope of reconciliation. A proper praying of "our Father" should drive toward redemption and reconciliation. The question, then, is how the language can be heard "properly."

The topic deserves attention at a range and level beyond this or any other single essay.[1] My task here is to ask how a reading of the Prayer in its Gospel settings can help to shape that proper hearing.

A. The Father/The Son

In an essay entitled, "The Background of Jesus' Prayer in the Jewish Liturgical Tradition," Joseph Heinemann comments:

> No special importance should be attached to the fact that God is addressed as "Father" or as "Our Father" at the opening of Jesus' prayer—instead of the address, "Master" or "God," often used in Jewish private prayer. For in the request "Thy kingdom come," which follows immediately, the alternative concept, expressed in the metaphor of "the servant before his king," is clearly implied.[2]

While his observations about the interchangability of language in Jewish tradition may be correct, patterns of usage in Matthew and Luke do not justify his view that the use of "Father" and "our Father" to open the Prayer is of little note. Consider a few observations regarding the use of "Father" for God in Matthew and Luke-Acts.

1. The term "Father" is employed far more frequently in Matthew than in Luke-Acts. "Father" is used of God 45 times in Matthew, in Luke 16 times (including the double-bracketed "Father, forgive them"), in Acts 3 times.
2. In both Gospels, only Jesus refers to God as "Father." The pattern holds for Acts as well, where the only references to God as "Father" occur in narrative reminiscences of Jesus' words (Acts 1:4, 7; 2:33).
3. In Matthew, God is "your Father" 18 times (5 are singular, 13 plural; of the total, 15 occur in the Sermon on the Mount); in Luke, God is "your" Father only three times (6:36; 12:30, 32). The only occurrence of "our Father" is in Matthew's version of the Lord's Prayer (not in Luke's, where the Prayer opens with the simple vocative, "Father").

[1] I would call attention to a preliminary effort in this direction in the paper "I Believe in God the Father," which I prepared with Patrick Keifert, now published in *Horizons* 20 (1990): 39-60.

[2] "The Background of Jesus' Prayer in the Jewish Liturgical Tradition," in *The Lord's Prayer and Jewish Liturgy*, ed. J. J. Petuchowski and M. Brocke (New York: Seabury Press, 1978), p. 88.

4. In the majority of references, Jesus refers to God as "my Father" or "the Father." On two occasions (in Matthew and Luke) Jesus addresses God as "Father": In his prayer of thanks that God has "hidden these things from the wise" (Mt. 11:25-27; Lk. 10:21-22) and in his Gethsemane prayer (Mt. 26:36-42; Lk. 22:39-42). (Interestingly, neither Matthew nor Luke employs the Aramaic "Abba" as does Mark.) Luke includes an additional address, namely in Jesus' last words, "Father, into your hands I commend my spirit" (Lk. 23:46).

Based on such statistics, one would have to say that reference to God as "Father" is uncommon and noteworthy. Jesus alone refers to God as Father—most commonly as "my Father" or as "the Father" (in relationship to "the Son"). The imagery derives at least in part from the royal tradition in the Psalms (see also 2 Sam. 7:14) where God addresses the king as "son." The scriptural overtones are particularly clear in Luke-Acts, where Psalm 2:7 not only underlies the account of Jesus' baptism and transfiguration, but is actually quoted in Acts 13:33 (Paul's speech in Antioch of Pisidia).[3] Father/son imagery is appropriate to the relationship between God and Jesus the Messiah.

Many of the occurrences of the imagery, however, particularly the use of the definite "the Father" and "the Son," cannot be derived from royal tradition. Only Jesus actually addresses God as "Father" in prayer, again most strikingly in Luke where he prays to God as "Father" on the Mount of Olives just prior to his arrest (22:42) and addresses God with his last words, "Father, into your hands I commit my spirit" (Lk. 23:46). Explanations of the derivation of the imagery may reasonably appeal to Jesus' own use of "Abba" in addressing God. Important for our study of the Lord's Prayer in Matthew and Luke is that Jesus' references to "my Father" and "the Father/the Son" do not invite imitation. Jesus is not a "typical" child of God. Others may use the language by invitation, not imitation. Only Jesus can refer to God as "your Father" (particularly in Matthew); only Jesus invites his followers to address God as "Father" in prayer.

Particularly striking is the complete absence of "Father" as a divine epithet in Acts (except in the references to Jesus' words in 1:4, 7; 2:33). No one refers to God as "Father"; no one ever addresses God as "Father" in prayer. For Luke, father/son imagery is employed almost exclusively to speak about

---

[3] The presence of royal overtones has been detected by other commentators. For a discussion, see chapter 3 of my *Messianic Exegesis* (Philadelphia: Fortress Press, 1988).

the relationship between God and Jesus. The extension of the imagery to include others is clearly derived from the primary relationship.

B. "Our Father"

While father/son imagery is employed first to speak of the relationship between God and Jesus, there are several instances—apart from the Lord's Prayer—where Jesus uses familial imagery to shed light on the relationship between the faithful and "our Father" (Mt. 6:25-33/Lk. 12:22-34; Mt. 7:7-11/Lk. 11:9-13). Jesus explicitly uses the image of a child asking a father for something to speak about the relationship to God in prayer (Mt. 7:9-11). These passages have a bearing on how the "Father" language is to be heard.

In the parable of the prodigal (Lk. 15:11-32), the relationship of the imagery to God is complex. Jeremias, among others, has argued that the parable is central to understanding what it means to call God "Father." Yet the parable does not function in Luke as a simple allegory. Jesus tells the story to shed light on his practice of receiving sinners and tax collectors in response to the grumbling of the scribes and Pharisees (Lk. 15:1-2). And while the image of God as father and Israel as son is familiar from the scriptures, such traditions form only the larger setting within which the imagery is heard. Jesus' parable has a logic of its own that explains the cast of characters. The parable has to do with rights of inheritance in which only fathers and sons would be involved. The theological thrust of the parable depends upon its being heard in the larger setting of Luke's Gospel and is best dealt with at some length (see below).

Perhaps the most suggestive passages, most closely related to the relationship to God in prayer, are the two which encourage the faithful to trust that their "Father" cares for them. In the first, the exhortation to have no anxiety is based on observations of nature, where the care of the creator (= your Heavenly Father [Mt.] or your Father [Lk.]) is presumed to be obvious in the order and beauty of the world. The second (Mt. 7:7-11/Lk. 11:9-13) develops the imagery of the Lord's Prayer. In Matthew, the invitation, "Ask, and it will be given you" (7:7) recalls the verse that introduces the Lord's Prayer: "for your Father knows what you need before you ask him" (6:8). While the rhetorical question, "Is there anyone among you who, if your child asks for bread, will give a stone?" (7:9) is addressed to parents, not simply fathers, the parental image of father chosen to speak of God is taken from the Lord's Prayer. The same is true in Luke, where the extended exhortation to be persistent in prayer serves as commentary on the Lord's

Prayer (11:2-4). Luke develops the Prayer to God as Father by encouraging perseverance in prayer, which is illustrated by playing on reasonable expectations both of friends (Lk. 11:5-8) and of fathers (11:9-13).

While Jesus must invite his followers to address God as "Father," he can appeal to ordinary human experience as a way of giving substance to the image of "Father." In fact, however, that appeal to natural human relations and to parental instincts bears little real weight in the narrative. More critical for understanding how to pray to God as "Father"—more critical, that is, for experiencing God as "Father"—is the key relationship in the story between "the Father" and "the Son."

C. God the Father/Jesus the Son

Perhaps it is obvious, but it is worth stating that the Gospels seek to offer an "argument" about God that assumes the form of a narrative. The Lord's Prayer is an aspect of the whole, and the weight of the narrative argument that provides its setting has to do with the relationship between God and Jesus, the Son of God. The Gospels claim that God's kingdom—God's reign and will—is tied to the ministry of Jesus who died and was vindicated on the third day. While there may be precedent in Jewish prayers and in nature for addressing God as "Father," the Gospels do not argue from nature or tradition to provide a sufficient basis for making requests of God the "Father in heaven." If there is reason for such confidence, it must be in light of what occurred between "the Father" and "the Son."

In what sense is God understood as Jesus' "Father," and what reasons do the Gospels offer for confidence that God can be our "Father"? In two of the most poignant passages in Luke, Jesus is "the Son" who prayed, "Father, if you are willing, remove this cup from me; yet not my will but yours be done" (Lk. 22:42). At his death, he prayed, "Father, into your hands I commend my spirit" (Lk. 23:46). Can God be trusted? The answer to this question has everything to do with what became of Jesus and his cause. And that is precisely the theme of the apostolic preaching in Acts: "This man, handed over to you by the definite plan and foreknowledge of God, you crucified and killed. . . . But God raised him up. . . . Repent, and be baptized every one of you in the name of Jesus Christ so that your sins may be forgiven" (Acts 2:22-38). We are invited to place our confidence in God who raised Jesus from the dead. At one level, Jesus can be understood as the test case. The story offers testimony that God "did not abandon his Holy One to

Hades" but raised him up. And it offers that testimony by arguing that what God has done in Jesus is "in accordance with the scriptures."

Jesus is not simply an example, however, but the Son whom God sent to be a blessing (Acts 3:26). We are invited to experience God as Father not simply because we have information about what it means to be a model child of God, not even because we are familiar with the details of Jesus' story, but because in Jesus' name the good news is offered to us by those who are commissioned like the apostles to preach. In Jesus' name we are called to repent, and our sins are forgiven. The story of Jesus warrants the preaching of God's word that does what it promises, and it is in light of this doing that we are invited to address God as "Father."

Let me bring all this back to the initial concern with the image of "Father." I do not wish to underestimate the degree to which traditional Christian language has been and can be alienating. Human relationships at their best serve only as limited analogies by which to understand our relationship to God. The brokenness of those relationships can render intimate metaphors virtually powerless—or even destructive. But we have no other language by which to address God than our own, and to eliminate the relational and intimate language of the tradition would be to deprive the church of its ability to address God in prayer.

I suggest that understanding the setting of the Lord's Prayer in Luke-Acts and Matthew's Gospel locates the scandal of the language and its promise in the right place. Calling God "our Father" has to do not primarily with traditional or "natural" imagery. We do not pray to God as "Male"; we do not speak of God as "Father" because of some natural necessity—e.g., a "natural law" according to which the cosmos is ordered according to gender distinctions. The God to whom we are invited to pray is known only in the particular—as the God whom Jesus addressed as "Father" and who vindicated the crucified Jesus as Christ, Son of God, by raising him from the dead. We experience God as "our Father" through Jesus. The words must be heard in their Gospel setting. The particularity of that setting (e.g., that Jesus actually called God "Father" and taught his followers to pray to God as "[our] Father") is the only promise of deliverance from ideologies of any sort that oppress and enslave and finally undermine the possibility of addressing God as one who cares and can be trusted to listen.

III. The "We" in the Lord's Prayer

I have spent a good bit of time reflecting on how we are to hear and to pray the opening words of the Lord's Prayer by hearing them in their Gos-

pel setting. I seem unable to get beyond those first words. I am struck by
the use of the first plural, not just the "our" in the opening address but
throughout the prayer. Who are "we"? "We" who are invited to pray to
"our Father" are a particular audience. Our lives have been shaped by a
political and cultural experiment whose achievements have been purchased
at a great price. In our culture, we are taught to think of ourselves more as
individuals than as social beings. Religion, like other matters of value, has
been relegated to the private realm: it is "my" business and no one else's.
The high value our culture places on tolerance effectively hinders the pursuit of shared values other than the right to believe what we choose. It is
symptomatic that we seem unable to produce leaders capable of capturing
public imagination so as to create a community of conviction, whether in
the area of religion or politics. Is the first person plural in the Lord's Prayer
thus nothing more than an empty grammatical remnant from another age?
Or worse, is it a slogan that establishes boundaries between a "we" and a
"they"? I want to argue that one of the things we can hear when we read
the Lord's Prayer in its New Testament settings is a grappling with this
question—and a promise that the Prayer has power to create an "us" from
God's scattered and alienated children.

While the experience of isolation and fragmentation may be more intense
in this society than in others, it is surely not new. The early chapters in
Genesis, which form the backdrop to God's special involvement in human
affairs that begins with the call of Abraham, chronicle the collapse of family
and social structures that results from sin. Brother is pitted against brother,
family against family, with the result that the human race is scattered across
the face of the earth, unable to communicate with one another, alienated
from the natural world. The New Testament is not naive with respect to
the power that alienates one from another; Jesus' story, after all, climaxes in
a crucifixion. But the gospel is a move toward reconciliation that God has
undertaken—reconciliation between earth and heaven and reconciliation
among the human family. Against the backdrop of the story of Babel,
Luke's account of Pentecost highlights a word that all can hear and understand in their own tongues, a word that spells the birth of a new possibility
for gathering together the scattered family of Israel—and eventually of "all
flesh."

The Lord's Prayer should be heard in the context of a story that is about
conflict, alienation, and reconciliation. The coming of the kingdom and the
establishing of God's will for which we are to pray has as one of its most
significant features the building of a community that can pray "Our Fa-

ther," "Give us our bread," "Forgive us our sins, as we forgive those who sin against us." The placement of the petition for forgiveness, coupled with recognition of forgiveness as something basic to the way we deal with one another, deserves attention not only because of its appropriateness to our setting but because it is a theme developed in each of the Gospels.

The emphasis is particularly clear in Matthew, where the verses immediately following the Lord's Prayer call attention to the petition for forgiveness, highlighting its social dimensions: "For if you forgive others their trespasses, your heavenly Father will also forgive you; but if you do not forgive others, neither will your Father forgive your trespasses" (Mt. 6:14-15).[4] God's forgiveness has social consequences; "the Father" is invested in the well-being of a community.

The instructions Jesus gives his followers in Matthew 18 serve as a kind of commentary on the command to forgive one another. The chapter spells out in some detail the efforts to which the faithful should go to seek reconciliation. Not a single "little one" is to be despised. Like a shepherd with a hundred sheep who diligently seeks out the one who is lost, members of the community should seek out those who have strayed. Instructions about disciplining someone who has sinned against another provide every opportunity for repentance and reconciliation (18:15-17); the faithful must be willing to forgive other "brothers" seventy times seven. That what drives the whole enterprise is the extraordinary mercy of God is made clear in the parable of the unforgiving servant (18:23-35). What God has forgiven is unimaginably great. Readers of the parable thus experience the absurdity of the servant's inability to remit even a small debt when he had been forgiven a fortune.

The community that prays to "our Father" for forgiveness lives by forgiveness and reconciliation that occur within the human family.

To say that is to say the obvious. Jesus' contemporaries would not have disagreed, and I suspect few civilized people would today. The language of forgiveness is not new to Jesus or the Christian tradition. Repentance and forgiveness had a place in traditional Jewish piety. John the Baptist preaches a "baptism of repentance for the forgiveness of sins" (Lk. 3:3 [as his father Zechariah prophesies in 1:77]). What is it, then, that makes this prayer interesting, more than a statement of the obvious? What indication is there that the forgiveness requested from God will result in a community in which forgiveness becomes a way of life and that can pray to "our" Father?

---

[4] Krister Stendahl called attention to the relationship between prayer and forgiveness in "Prayer and Forgiveness," *Svensk exegetisk årsbok* 22-23 (1957-58): 74-86.

One crucial matter is how God actually forgives sins. At issue in the Gospels is not whether sins can be forgiven by God but that Jesus presumes the right to speak for God. He not only speaks about forgiveness but declares sins forgiven (Mt. 9:2-8; Lk. 5:17-26). And he gives his disciples a similar authority. According to Matthew, he authorizes them to bind and loose sins (Mt. 18:18-20); in Luke he commissions his disciples to proclaim repentance and forgiveness of sins in his [the Messiah's = Jesus'] name (Lk. 24:47). That presumption strikes pious Jews as blasphemous. At issue is whether "the Son of man has authority to forgive sins."

That authority to forgive sins likewise involves determining who will be forgiven and what will be required of them. Jesus' association with "sinners and tax collectors" threatens traditional piety. And because that issue of authority is central to the conflict that drives the story of Jesus' ministry toward the final confrontation in Jerusalem, it is not a small matter that it is Jesus who teaches the disciples to pray "Forgive us our sins" and to address God as "Father." The prayer is his prayer—the Lord's Prayer; its authority depends upon Jesus' authorization.

While it may not be obvious in the wording of the Lord's Prayer, the Prayer in its Gospel settings should be heard and prayed with a christological focus. The prayer for forgiveness, like the address of God as "Father," is tied to the confession of Jesus as the crucified and risen Christ, Son of God. Jesus commissions his followers to preach repentance and forgiveness of sins. To the language familiar to Jewish tradition is appended a distinctive feature: repentance and forgiveness of sins are announced "in Jesus' name." Luke-Acts offers some sense of why it is in Jesus' name that we should expect to encounter a gracious God (an enterprise that includes learned interpretation of the scriptures, like the demonstration in Peter's first speech that the promise from Joel, "Whoever calls on the name of the Lord will be saved" [Acts 2:21 quoting Joel 2:32], refers to the "Lord" Jesus), and the story traces new ventures in community that spring up from this particular experience of forgiveness.

Such christological particularity influences how we are to understand the "sins" for which we ask forgiveness. In the early speeches in Acts, the apostolic preaching takes shape, and the message of repentance and forgiveness is given a particular focus. The "sin" for which Peter urges the crowds to repent in his opening speeches is the killing of Jesus (Acts 2:22-23, 37-38; 3:14-20). There are instances in Acts where sin is portrayed in traditional Jewish terms (e.g., greed and dishonesty in 5:1-11; false prophecy in 13:6-12; idolatry in 14:15-16 and 17:24-26). The matter in which the narrative invests the most, however, is the sin of unbelief.[5] God's gracious work is now tied to apostolic preaching and to faith "in Jesus' name" ("Whoever calls on the name of the Lord [Jesus] will be saved" [Acts 2:21, quoting Joel 2:32]).

And the Jesus in whom faith is urged is the one who was crucified. His practice of forgiveness and healing did not lead to the building of a community among his contemporaries but to fragmentation and bloodshed. Praying Jesus' prayer to "the Father," in which we ask for forgiveness, requires some experience of the scandal of that cross in order to realize its promise.

A. "The Christ Must Suffer"

In Luke, Jesus' suffering and death are described as "necessary": "the Christ must suffer" (Lk. 24:26, 46). The Gospel story offers a narrative argument for that necessity.

In his ministry, Jesus has little difficulty with "sinners." They flock to him. Their diseases are healed, their demons driven out, and their sins forgiven. Central to that ministry to sinners are the table scenes in Luke, where Jesus welcomes the unwashed who have no reason to expect a place at his table. Something happens to those with whom Jesus sits at table. A sinful woman has her sins forgiven (7:36-50); Zacchaeus makes a radical change in his life (19:1-10); the Emmaus travellers recognize Jesus' risen presence only when they break bread with him (24:13-35). It makes a great difference, therefore, who will be allowed at the table.

The controversy surrounding table fellowship in the Gospel and in Acts is thus not a minor issue. It is precisely Jesus' table practices that offend. The righteous find his willingness to eat with sinners and tax collectors symptomatic of a careless disregard of the law—God's law—by which life is to be ordered. They recognize—rightly—that his behavior is dangerous. His affection for sinners and his careless generosity with places at his table may undermine the whole moral and religious structure by which society is sustained. The bread for which Jesus urges his disciples to pray is to be eaten with others. But what will be the conditions for that eating?

B. The Lament of a Responsible Child (Lk. 15:11-32)

The problem takes shape in the story Jesus tells about a father and his two sons, a parable identified by other commentators as crucial for under-

---

[5] In Luke's Gospel, Jesus' warning about "sin against the Holy Spirit" is tied to rejection of the apostolic preaching which is inspired by the Spirit, who even provides speech for those obliged to give testimony (Lk. 12:8-12).

standing what it means to pray to God as "Father." The parable, usually known as "the parable of the prodigal son" (or "the parable of the waiting father"), should more aptly be titled, "the lament of a responsible child." It is told in response to the grumbling of scribes and Pharisees about Jesus' practice of eating with tax collectors and sinners (15:1-2). The parable takes their protest far more seriously than do most commentators. Jesus' willingness to welcome to his table those whose lives demonstrate contempt for God's law conjures up the real possibility of undermining moral seriousness and determination. The possibility of bringing all of life under the sacred canopy of God's law is threatened by actions that suggest God is not serious about the law.

Consider the parable. It has been customary to argue that the younger child is the focus and that in his repentance and return home there is an example (better, an invitation) for all believers to do likewise. Yet the parable does little to allay the fears of those suspicious of sinners and cheats. The parable never says that the young profligate repents. It says only that he "comes to himself," which may well mean simply recognizing his desperate state. His carefully rehearsed speech ("Father, I have sinned against heaven and before you; I am not worthy to be called your son") may reflect a hunch, born of experience, that his doting father will latch onto those empty sentences like some hungry fish unable to resist the bait. While such a cynical reading of the parable may seem unwarranted, it is significant that the story does nothing to head off such a reading. To what extent is the image of a spineless, sentimental father unable to deny anything to his favorite, a suitable image for God? Addressing such a God as "Father" will hardly result in life-saving changes among the prodigals in our midst.

At least that is the view of the elder brother in the story, the only really interesting and sympathetic character. Notice how he is introduced: "Now his elder brother was in the field; and when he came and approached the house, he heard music and dancing" (15:25). The responsible member of the family is doing chores. No one has seen fit to tell him of the party already in progress. He must ask one of the servants to learn of the celebration. He has been at his work, after all, without which the farm would cease to function. The father's preoccupation with the young profligate sweeps away all concern for the well-being of the family, taking the responsible child for granted. The elder brother's protest gathers up all the resentment of responsible people, who have committed themselves to holding off the chaos that threatens to sweep away civilized life and expect nothing more than justice, in the form of an eloquent lament: "You have never given me even a goat."

It is as if irresponsible behavior is rewarded. There are no safeguards to insure that repentance is genuine, no efforts to affirm the responsible. There is no justice, the elder child complains, and without it the whole human enterprise will collapse. Jesus' religious critics were correct to see him as a threat to religion and morality.

The parable does not end with the lament, however. It concludes with poignant words of the father that raise the problem to another level. "Your brother was dead and is alive again." Can't you rejoice? Isn't that worth a party? Can't you understand the risk I must take for the sake of restoring your brother to our family? Can't you come in and have a bite with us?

The questions, which are left unanswered in the parable, receive their answer in the narrative. The elder brothers are not convinced; the pious are not persuaded. They cannot risk the graciousness embodied in Jesus' ministry—a graciousness, we are to know, that characterizes the reign of God. Though Jesus can provide bread enough for all and everyone is invited to the table, they will not come. They are powerless to move and incapable of rejoicing in the deliverance Jesus accomplishes among the outcasts. And when the moment comes to choose between Jesus and the traditional safeguards, both religious and political, the responsible members of Jewish and Roman society have no choice but to put Jesus to death.

How shall responsible children pray to God as "Father"? Such a prayer is unthinkable as long as bitterness and smoldering resentment can be rekindled by the very graciousness that allows a place for prodigals. Such a prayer is possible only if liberation of another sort can be experienced—only if bondage to resentment can be broken, a bondage that masks itself as virtue and concern for justice. The elder children will be able to ask for forgiveness and extend it to others only if God's forgiveness extends to them, the pious and the responsible, as well as to the sinners and tax collectors, whose sin is the inability to forgive God for being gracious to the ungodly.

This is precisely how apostolic preaching is cast in Acts. It is addressed to all those implicated in Jesus' death: "You killed him . . . but God raised him up." God's raising of Jesus from the dead is a refusal to accept rejection as the final word. It becomes the occasion for offering forgiveness to those who would never have imagined themselves to be sinful—and whose bondage is thus the more desperate. The preaching of that message offers the possibility of experiencing a graciousness that can open to a different form of life together. "Forgive us our sins, for we too forgive everyone indebted to us" (NRSV); "Forgive us our sins, for we too forgive everyone who does wrong to us" (Fitzmyer).[6] The respectable and the pious must learn how to forgive both "sinners" and a God whose graciousness threatens their way of ordering the world, and that is possible only because God will not be put off even by rejection.

Thus the message that God raised Jesus from the dead becomes for such people a "message of repentance and forgiveness"—but only through an experience of the cross. The discovery that there is no alternative for us but resentment and suspicion becomes an occasion for deliverance not unlike an experience of death and life, to use Paul's imagery (Rom. 6:13). Or to use an image from Flannery O'Conner, forgiveness will be experienced by the responsible as the "burning away even of our virtues."[7] Such imagery is quite appropriate to Luke's "baptism with the Holy Spirit and fire" (Lk. 3:16). The gospel's promise is that the burning results in new beings fit to sit at the banquet table.

According to Acts, faith in the promise of God's forgiveness "in Jesus' name" results in a community that can understand itself as "we" and even understand its possessions as "ours." It can pray for "our daily bread," recognizing that when it is broken together in Jesus' name, the Lord is present and we can enjoy a foretaste of God's domain, fulfilling the desire of the creator for rebuilding the fragmented human family.

The Gospel stories of Matthew and Luke-Acts provide the setting within which the Lord's Prayer is heard and prayed. The stories serve as access to a reign of God in which we are delivered from bondage to private experience, resentment, and alienation. The praying of the "Our Father," in a setting where that gospel story is rehearsed, where forgiveness is declared, and where people break bread together at the Lord's table, will serve not only as an indicator of what God wills but as an agency in the establishing of God's reign.

[6] J. A. Fitzmyer, *The Gospel According to Luke (X-XXIV): Introduction, Translation, and Notes*, The Anchor Bible, vol. 28A (Garden City: Doubleday & Co., 1985), p. 896.

[7] "Revelation," in *The Complete Stories* (New York: Farrar, Straus, Giroux, 1971), p. 508.

The Lord's Prayer in Patristic Literature

by Karlfried Froehlich

I

Jules Lebreton once said that the Lord's Prayer was the biblical text most commented upon in ancient Christian literature. Indeed, it is hard to find any author who does not remark upon, or at least allude to, these few biblical verses somewhere in the course of his extant works. There is also an astonishing amount of substantial commentary from fathers and church writers East and West.[1] In the East, the foundational piece was Origen's exposition of the Lord's Prayer in his treatise "On Prayer" (233/34).[2] Gregory of Nyssa used this work extensively in five profound homilies "On the Lord's Prayer" which he preached in his mature years (after 379) and which remained popular reading for centuries to come.[3] We also have running commentaries in Cyril of Jerusalem's "Fifth Mystagogical Catechesis" from the middle of the fourth century;[4] Theodore of Mopsuestia's "Eleventh Catechetical Homily" of 388/92;[5] John Chrysostom's Commentary on Matthew;[6] and Cyril of Alexandria's biblical commentary on the Gospel of Luke.[7] In the West, the list is even longer.[8] The earliest and most influential

---

[1] For a survey in English, see G. W. H. Lampe, " 'Our Father' in the Fathers," in *Christian Spirituality: Essays in Honour of Gordon Rupp*, ed. P. Brooks (London: SCM Press, 1975), pp. 11-31.

[2] Greek text: GCS *Origenes* 2, ed. P. Koetschau (1899), pp. 297-403; English translation: *Alexandrian Christianity*, ed. J. E. Oulton and H. Chadwick, The Library of Christian Classics, vol. 2 (Philadelphia: Westminster Press, 1954), pp. 238-387. In the bibliographical notes, I am using the standard abbreviations for series in which patristic texts are published. They are listed, e.g., in J. Quasten et al., *Patrology*, vols. 1-4 (Westminster: Christian Classics, 1962-1986).

[3] Greek text: PG 44, 1120-1193; English translation: Hilda C. Graef, ACW 18 (1954), pp. 21-84.

[4] Greek text: *Sources Chrétiennes* 126 (1966), ed. A. Piédagnel and P. Paris, pp. 160-168; English translation: L. P. McCauley and A. Stephenson, FC 64 (1970), pp. 198-202.

[5] Syriac text with French translation: R. Tonneau and R. Devreesse, *Les homélies catéchétiques de Théodore de Mopsuestia*, Studi e Testi, 145 (Rome, 1949), pp. 281-321: English translation: A. Mingana, *Commentary of Theodore of Mopsuestia on the Lord's Prayer and on the Sacraments of Baptism and the Eucharist*, Woodbrooke Studies, 6 (Cambridge: Heffer, 1933), pp. 1-16.

[6] Greek text: PG 57, 278-283; English translation: NPNF, ser. 1, vol. 10, pp. 134-137.

[7] English translation (1859) of the Syriac text: R. Payne Smith, *St. Cyril of Alexandria: Commentary on the Gospel of Luke* (n.p.: Studion Publishers, 1983), pp. 297-320.

[8] See the recent monograph by K. B. Schnurr, *Hören und Handeln: Lateinische Auslegungen*

expositions were Part 1 of Tertullian's treatise *On Prayer*, written just around 200 A.D.,[9] and a treatise *On the Lord's Prayer* which Cyprian wrote at the beginning of the Decian persecution in 250.[10] Ambrose of Milan explained the Lord's Prayer as part of his mystagogical catecheses of ca. 390/91 which are preserved in his *De sacramentis*.[11] From Augustine's hand we have the early commentary in his "Exposition of the Lord's Sermon on the Mount" written between 392 and 396;[12] a wonderfully rich treatment in his pastoral Letter 130 to the widow Proba, a noblewoman from Rome who had fled to North Africa from the invading Visigoths in 410;[13] a catechetical exposition in Sermons 56-59 from about the same time;[14] and an anti-Pelagian interpretation in the late treatise *On the gift of perseverance* (429/30) in which he makes ample use of Cyprian's classical exposition as proof of his thesis that perseverance is a free gift from God and is a central theme of all petitions.[15] From the first half of the fifth century we also have brief remarks in Jerome's commentary on the Gospel of Matthew;[16] full expositions in John Cassian's "Conferences" (IX.18-24);[17] the poet Sedulius' "Easter Hymn" (II, 231-300) and its prose version in the *Paschale Opus* (II, 17);[18] the fourteenth homily of the anonymous *Opus imperfectum in Matthaeum*;[19] six sermons (nos. 67-72) of Petrus Chrysologus, bishop of Ravenna,[20] and several anonymous homilies going under the names of Augustine, Chrysostom, and Quodvultdeus.[21]

---

des Vaterunsers in der Alten Kirche bis zum fünften Jahrhundert, Freiburger Theologische Studien, 132 (Freiburg: Herder, 1985).

[9] Latin text: CCL 1 (1954), ed. G. F. Diercks, pp. 257-263; English translation: R. Arbesmann, FC 40 (1959), pp. 157-168.

[10] Latin text: CCL 3A (1976), ed. C. Moreschini, pp. 88-113; English translation: R. J. Deferrari, FC 36 (1958), pp. 127-159.

[11] *De sacramentis* V.4.18-30. Latin text: CSEL 73 (1955), ed. O. Faller, pp. 65-72; English translation: R. J. Deferrari, FC 44 (1963), pp. 314-318.

[12] Latin text: CCL 35 (1967), ed. A. Mutzenbecher, pp. 99-131; English translation: J. J. Jepsen, ACW 5 (1948), pp. 100-127.

[13] Latin text: CSEL 44 (1904), ed. A. Goldbacher, pp. 40-77; English translation: W. Parsons, FC 18 (1958), pp. 376-401.

[14] Latin text: PL 38, 377-402; English translation: NPNF, ser. 1, vol. 6, pp. 274-289.

[15] Latin text: PL 45, 993-999; English translation: NPNF, ser. 1, vol. 5, pp. 526-529.

[16] Latin text: CCL 77 (1969), ed. D. Hurst and M. Adriaen, pp. 36-37; no English translation.

[17] Latin text: CSEL 13 (1886), ed. M. Petschenig, pp. 265-272; English translation: C. Luibheid, *John Cassian: Conferences*, CWS (New York: Paulist Press, 1985), pp. 111-116.

[18] Latin text: PL 19, 622-634; English translation: G. Sigerson (Dublin, 1922). I was unable to consult this translation.

[19] Latin text (under the name of John Chrysostom): PG 56, 711-715; no English translation.

[20] Latin text: CCL 24A (1981), ed. A. Olivar, pp. 402-444; English translation: G. E. Ganss, FC 17 (1953), pp. 115-123 (partial).

[21] Schnurr, *Hören und Handeln*, pp. 234-276.

Traces of the Lord's Prayer and its interpretation can, of course, be found much earlier. Context and wording in the Gospels of Matthew and Luke reflect not only use but also interpretation. Among the Apostolic Fathers, allusions have been claimed to be present in 1 Clement (13:3; 34:5; 60:2-3) as well as Polycarp's Epistle (6:1-2; 7:2) and his Martyrdom (7:1), and the full quotation of the text in Didache 8:2 has posed a considerable challenge to exegetes and historians. While the context of the Didache passage with its sections on baptism, fasting, praying, and the eucharistic meal reflects a polemic against "judaizing dissidents" in the church or churches addressed,[22] it also underscores the strong Jewish matrix of the prayer. The final two-part doxology ("For yours is the power, and the glory"), absent in Matthew and Luke, appears again in the prayer formulas for the eucharistic service in Didache 9 and 10 (9:4; 10:5) where we also find the phrase, "our Father" (9:2); "bread," "kingdom" (9:4; 10:5); "your holy name" (10:2); and "salvation from all evil" (10:5). The Jewish roots of all these prayers cannot be doubted, and the variations in the transmitted texts of the Lord's Prayer—the Didache version is close to Matthew but deviates at four points—are in themselves an indication of Jewish liturgical practice as its *Sitz im Leben*. One of these natural Jewish variations may be the doxology itself: Jewish prayers frequently had a freely formulated ending (*hotima*, seal) for which apparently one form became standard in the Christian use of the Lord's Prayer in the second century.

How early is the evidence for such a general use of the Lord's Prayer in the Christian churches? The question received new urgency with the discovery of a possible Christian reading of the famous magical square SATOR AREPO in 1926.[23] The square, formed by the five words SATOR AREPO TENET OPERA ROTAS, can be read as a cryptogram spelling two times PATERNOSTER, the beginning of the "Our Father" in Latin, in the form of a cross, with the "N" as the cross point and the letters A and O added twice on both sides. The presence of the square in four locations at Pompeii would force one to assume that the prayer was already well known in Italy in its Latin translation as early as 79 A.D., that is, at a time when the language of Christians in Rome was still Greek and their number outside Rome was very small. I would side with the scholars who regard the square

[22] A. Tuilier, "Didache," in *Theologische Realenzyklopädie* (Berlin and New York: Walter de Gruyter, 1981), vol. 8, p. 733.

[23] See H. Last, "The Rotas-Sator Square: Present Positions and Future Prospects," *Journal of Theological Studies*, n.s. 3 (1952): 92-97; W. O. Moeller, *The Mithraic Origin and Meanings of the Rotas-Sator Square*, Etudes préliminaires aux religions orientales, 38 (Leiden: Brill, 1973), esp. pp. 44-52 (bibliography).

as pre-Christian, dissolvable as a cryptogram into other word sequences (e.g., PATER-N-SOTER), so that it does not tell us anything about the early Christian use of the Lord's Prayer. Its possible Christian reading may explain to some extent, however, why the square continued to enjoy such success later on, even though no patristic writer ever refers to the PATER-NOSTER reading.

II

The reason for the wide diffusion of the Lord's Prayer in the Late Roman Empire was certainly not that it was a favorite biblical passage. Rather, the underlying prayer itself, short, succinct, and covered by the authority of the Christian "lawgiver," had a tremendous potential in the popular prayer culture of the time in which the superstitious use of powerful prayer formulae was rampant. Just as the occurrences of the SATOR AREPO square at Pompeii and elsewhere point to the use of such verbal devices in the context of magic and incantation, so the text of the "Our Father" is found (at least later) on the accessories of superstitious popular piety such as scraps of parchment, lamps or amulets, serving as a talisman or a guarding charm.

For Christian theologians, the framework of the text of the Lord's Prayer in the Gospels gave it additional significance. The use of the "Our Father" among Christians was a command of Christ: "Pray then like this" (Mt. 6:9); "When you pray, say" (Lk. 11:2). The framing words do not indicate what kind of use was intended—use in private prayer or in the communal worship setting. Origen noted the differences between the Matthean and the Lukan form and concluded that the two settings, one a public ordinance, the other the answer to a private request, indicated that these were two different prayers with a number of common elements. The quotation in Didache 8:2 is followed by the injunction: "Three times daily you shall pray in this manner." While the rule of "three times daily" seems to imply a private prayer discipline according to Jewish custom, the addition of the *hotima* suggests the setting of communal prayer which is the subject of discussion in the following chapters. Some patristic authors lay great stress on the communal use. Their warrant is the text itself. It says, "*Our* Father," not "*My* Father" (Cyprian; Chrysostom). Clearly, very early already and even more so later on, the central *Sitz im Leben* of the Lord's Prayer was in the worship of the congregation while we hear little of its use in private devotion before the late third and early fourth centuries.

Cyprian linked his interpretation of the address, "Our Father," to the experience of reciting the Lord's Prayer at baptism: "As soon as people believe in his [Christ's] name and have become children of God, they must begin by giving thanks and professing themselves as children of God by calling God their father in heaven" (chap. 9). They also must "give witness with the very first words after their rebirth that they renounce their earthly, carnal father" (ibid.). Cyprian seems to imply that the first public recitation of the Lord's Prayer by newly baptized Christians occurred immediately after their baptism, presumably when they joined the congregation in the celebration of the eucharist for the first time. From Augustine's writings we can reconstruct the somewhat more elaborate sequence of the preparation for baptism in the North African church of the fourth century. People who asked to be "enrolled" received first the catechetical instructions for *competentes* which culminated in the teaching of the creed and its public recitation (*traditio* and *redditio symboli*) during Lent. The Lord's Prayer was taught on the Saturday before the fifth Sunday in Lent ("Judica") and recited one week later on the eve of Palm Sunday (*redditio orationis*).[24]

The passage from Cyprian strongly suggests that his church knew the use of the Lord's Prayer in the eucharistic liturgy as well. The first explicit mention of this practice, however, occurs with Cyril of Jerusalem in the middle of the fourth century. The step-by-step description of the eucharistic celebration in Cyril's fifth "mystagogical homily" places the "Our Father" after the *Praefatio* and the Great Thanksgiving with *epiclesis* and intercessions, immediately before the dialogue, "Holy things for the holy"—"One is holy, one is the Lord, Jesus Christ," and the communion. In recent scholarship, the thesis that such a use of the prayer goes far back, perhaps into apostolic times, has been vigorously defended, not only by Roman Catholics and Anglicans but also by Reformed scholars. Willy Rordorf even suggested that variations of the verb tense in the manuscript tradition of the fifth petition might reflect liturgical practice: Different from the present tense, *aphiomen* or *aphiemen* (Lk.; Western mss of Mt.), the aorist in Matthew, *aphēkamen*, seems to presuppose a separate act of reconciliation before the praying of the "Our Father" at the eucharist.[25] Such early use at the eucharist, however, is doubted by others.[26] They point to the fact that the earliest accounts of eucharistic celebrations such as Justin Martyr and Hippolytus do not mention the recitation of the "Our Father" among the prayers.

We know little about the use of the Lord's Prayer in early monastic com-

---

[24] Schnurr, *Hören und Handeln*, pp. 111-112.

[25] W. Rordorf, "Wie auch wir vergeben *haben* unsern Schuldnern (Matth. VI, 12b)," in *Studia Patristica*, ed. F. L. Cross (Berlin: Akademie-Verlag, 1970), vol. 10, pp. 236-241.

[26] F. E. Vokes, "The Lord's Prayer in the First Three Centuries," ibid., pp. 253-260.

munities. Traditional Benedictine practice gave it a place in all the monastic hours. Balthasar Fischer has suggested that its inclusion may have been meant as a recollection of one's baptism and that the practice of silent recitation at compline is a remnant of the Prayer's original use in private devotion.[27]

III

We owe most of the surviving patristic expositions of the Lord's Prayer to its liturgical use, especially in the context of baptism. Many of them were preached as catechetical homilies either preceding the *translatio orationis* as in North Africa, or following it during Easter week as "mystagogical catecheses" as in the case of Milan and Jerusalem. This may explain the overwhelming emphasis on the Prayer's doctrinal and ethical content: The "Our Father" was seen as a text teaching in brief everything a Christian needed to know about the faith and Christian behavior. Tertullian praised it as *breviarium totius evangelii* (a short compend of the entire gospel). Some later writers marvelled at the wealth of theological content expressed in the address alone: "Our Father—to say these words means to confess one's faith in the forgiveness of sins, remission of punishment, justification, sanctification, redemption, adoption as a child of God, an heir, a sibling of the Only-Begotten, enjoying the communion of the Holy Spirit" (Chrysostom). The role of the "Our Father" in catechetical instruction made it inevitable to mine the short text for all its possible implications.

Chrysostom's exposition comes from his Matthew-commentary. Again, since the First Gospel was the primary source of the Gospel lessons in the liturgy, commentaries on Matthew are relatively numerous and yield some important exegetical treatments in extant sections on Mt. 6. Perhaps the most interesting group of patristic expositions of the Lord's Prayer, however, belongs in the context of apologetic literature. In their defense of Christian prayer in general, Christian writers reveal the deeper reasons for the relative cohesion of patristic exegesis of the "Our Father" as well as for much of its variety. A general assumption is shared with all religions: Prayer in its nature is first and foremost petition, the imploration of the deity for a favor or benefit. The problem obviously is the danger of attempting to strike a bargain with God, to manipulate the deity. In a thoughtful article some years ago, Don Capps has raised the question whether petitionary prayer is

[27] B. Fischer, "Formen privater Tauferinnerung im Abendland: Das Herrengebet als Tauferinnerung," *Liturgisches Jahrbuch* 9 (1959): 161-162.

correctly understood if it is seen as a battle of wills—human vs. divine.[28] He prefers to describe it as an elemental act of communication. I would like to submit that this very insight is expressed in much of the patristic theology of prayer, most forcefully by Origen and Augustine.

IV

Origen's treatise on prayer is styled as the answer to some questions posed to him by his patron, Ambrose, and an otherwise unknown lady, Tatiana.

> Let the position be stated now in the very words of the letter you addressed to me. They are as follows: First, if God knows the future beforehand and it must come to pass, prayer is in vain. Secondly, if all things happen according to the will of God, and if what is willed by him is fixed, and nothing of what he wills can be changed, prayer is in vain.[29]

The letter perhaps contained the additional request for an exposition of the Lord's Prayer. In the second part of his treatise, Origen uses such an exposition to reenforce his general points, adding in a short third section some practical advice about time, location, and proper physical posture for prayer. His answer to the question asked by his correspondents begins with the central philosophical issue: free will. The very act of praying as an act of free will is foreseen and foreordained by God: "God uses to the full the free will of each thing upon earth."[30] "Each act of free will is adapted to such an arrangement of the whole as the settled order of the universe demands."[31]

In a recent monograph, Maria-Barbara v. Stritzky has clarified the philosophical context:[32] Stoic, Epicurean and Neoplatonic attitudes toward prayer were not uniform. Where prayer was criticized as "superfluous," the reason was a high, abstract view of a providential deity and its utterly transcendent nature; prayer cannot touch it. Still, the same authors often conceded a limited value of prayer in the realm of magic and theurgy and as the wordless expression of the intellectual worship of the *sophos*; the attitude of prayer can be an appropriate preparation for the inner ascent. Origen countered the criticism with the affirmation of Christian revelation: In Christ, God can be known and approached. "Through Christ," not to

---

[28] D. Capps, "The Psychology of Petitionary Prayer," *Theology Today* 39 (1982): 130-142.
[29] V.6. Oulton and Chadwick, *Alexandrian Christianity*, p. 250.
[30] VII.1; ibid., p. 254.
[31] VI.4; ibid., p. 252.
[32] M.-B. v. Stritzky, *Studien zur Überlieferung und Interpretation des Vaterunsers in der frühchristlichen Literatur*, Münsterische Beiträge zur Theologie, 57 (Münster i.W., 1989).

Christ, prayers can be, and should be, offered to God who is the giver of all knowledge but has made it clear that he wants to be asked. Origen also appropriated the philosophical argument about the limited value of prayer. Even if petitionary prayer were superfluous, there are always many benefits for the one who prays:

> If the calling to mind and reminiscence of an illustrious person who has profited by wisdom stirs us up to emulate him or her and often checks evil impulses, how much more does the calling to mind of God, the Father of the universe, together with prayer to him, benefit those who are confident in themselves that they stand before and speak to God as one who is present.[33]

We find the same line of argument in Augustine's writings. Discussing Mt. 6:8, Augustine raises the question, "Does it make sense to pray?" He answers: "Yes—the very effort we make in praying calms the heart, makes it clean, and renders it more capable of receiving the divine gifts which are poured out upon us in a spiritual manner. For God does not hear us because he seeks the favor of our prayers. . . . But *we* are not always prepared to receive."[34] Or: "We do not need words in dealing with God to obtain what we want; what matters are the things we carry in our minds and the direction of our thoughts, with pure love and single affection. The Lord made use of words to teach us those very things that by committing them to memory we may remember them at the time of prayer."[35] What should we ask for? God knows beforehand what we need (Mt. 6:8). In his *Letter to Proba*, Augustine answers very much like the philosophers: "Pray for the *beata vita*, the happy life. All humans desire it." That life will be God's final gift and will therefore remain the constant object of our longing as long as we are on earth: "When we pray with constant desire and exercise faith, hope, and charity, we 'pray always' (1 Thess. 5:17). Yet, at certain stated times and hours we also use words in prayer to God that we . . . may acquaint ourselves with the measure of progress we have made in this desire."[36] This indeed is the common conviction of patristic writers concerning prayer: God wants our prayer, verbal and attitudinal, but God does not need it. We pray not for God's benefit but for our own. *We* need this elemental act of communication.

[33] VIII.2; Oulton and Chadwick, *Alexandrian Christianity*, p. 255.
[34] *Sermon on the Mount* II.3.14; cf. Jepsen, ACW 5, p. 103.
[35] II.3.13; cf. ibid., pp. 102-103.
[36] Letter 130.4 and 9.

V

We noticed the central place of Mt. 6:8 in Augustine's argument. The foundational role of the biblical material in Origen's apology for prayer is even more striking. Practically all of his main points are unfolded as interpretations of specific biblical texts. The exegesis of an *agraphon*, "Ask for the great things, and the little things shall be added unto you" (cf. Mt. 6:8, 33) yields the central admonition that the content of prayer should not focus on this bodily life but on the heavenly things connected with our salvation.[37] 1 Thess. 5:17, "pray without ceasing," is exegeted in terms of prayer as the attitude of "tuning in" on God: "That person prays without ceasing . . . who combines with the prayer the needful deeds and the prayer with the fitting actions. For thus alone can we accept 'pray without ceasing' as a practicable saying, if we speak of the whole life of the saint as one great unbroken prayer of which that which is commonly called prayer is a part."[38] This understanding is connected with the injunction of verbal prayer three times a day citing the biblical example of Daniel (Dan. 6:10), Peter (Acts 10:9-10), and David (Ps. 5:3; 141:2). The book of Tobit allows Origen to infer that angelic beings close to God are engaged in enforcing and mediating our prayers before God (Tobit 3:16-17; 12:12),[39] and Ps. 123:1 ("To you I have lifted up my eyes, o you who dwells in heaven") teaches that the result of our praying is anagogy, the spiritual ascent of the soul to God.[40] Even the proper subdivisions of verbal prayer are inferred from a verse of the Bible: "Supplications, prayers, intercessions, thanksgivings" (1 Tim. 2:1). Ambrose, in the liturgical context of his mystagogical catechesis, changed the list to "praise, supplication, postulation, thanksgiving" and applied it to the seven parts of the Lord's Prayer.

VI

Modern exegetes note with some condescension the absence in the patristic interpretation of the Lord's Prayer of important exegetical insights such as a consideration of the Jewish background, the eschatological thrust of all the petitions as a prayer of Jesus, redactional differences between Matthew and Luke and their implications for variety among different early Christian communities, and other details. We have to keep in mind, however, the peculiar nature of patristic exegesis which showed less interest in the

[37] XIV.1; XVI.2; Oulton and Chadwick, *Alexandrian Christianity*, pp. 266, 272.
[38] XII.2; ibid., pp. 261-262.
[39] XI.1; ibid., p. 259.
[40] IX.2; XXIII.4; ibid., pp. 256, 285.

uniqueness of a passage than in its place within the unified biblical witness as a whole. It should not come as a surprise, therefore, that the interpretation of the Lord's Prayer and its single petitions was given its specific direction by other biblical texts which were widely shared as common reference points. Many of these texts owe their association with the "Our Father" to the liturgy, i.e., to the familiar lessons read at baptism or eucharist. The great prominence given to Rom. 10:13-15 in Augustine's Sermons 56-59, e.g., clearly derives from the Epistle lesson at the baptismal service. It seems to me that the various accents in the exegesis of particular petitions of the Lord's Prayer derive as much from the persuasive power of such biblical cross-references as from the philosophical and doctrinal emphases of an author's hermeneutical principles. One consequence is that a textual parallel between two interpretations does not necessarily indicate literary dependence. Modern authors show surprise at the relatively strong consensus which they discover among patristic interpretations of the Lord's Prayer at many points. Otto Dibelius, in his still valuable doctoral dissertation written under Harnack in 1902, found that the astonishing closeness of Luther's catechetical explanations of the Prayer to earlier vernacular texts has to be attributed not to direct borrowing but to a common source: the unified patristic tradition with its store of explanatory biblical keys.[41]

In discussing the patristic interpretation of the Lord's Prayer we must pay close attention to this store of passages adduced by the writers, especially the earliest ones whose work was likely to provide the foundation for a tradition on which later writers would draw. Often, these traditional cross-references steered the interpretation in a specific, sometimes surprising direction and might explain common emphases which we encounter time and again.

VII

a. Take the address, "Our Father." Today, many people question the implications of a gender-specific, exclusively male Father-God. It is easy to accuse the patristic writers of insensitivity at this point. As some feminist theologians have pointed out, our problem arose with the ideological hardening of an authoritarian father-image in a male-dominated culture which did not allow the different nuances of a much richer Jewish and Christian biblical God-talk to be heard and heeded. In a brilliant essay published in 1976 Antonie Wlosok demonstrated that it was Lactantius in the fourth

[41] O. Dibelius, *Das Vaterunser: Umrisse zu einer Geschichte des Gebets in der Alten und Mittleren Kirche* (Gießen, 1903).

century who adapted the image of the Christian God to a Constantinian ideology of *Dominus Pater ac Deus*, God Father Almighty, which politicized the older Roman notion of *patria potestas* in a one-sided, imperialistic direction and prepared the way for the political, cultural, and theological male absolutisms of later times.[42]

It is significant that, for patristic writers, the "Father" of the Lord's Prayer does not refer to a biological notion of fatherhood, even in the more abstract sense of origin or creatorship, but to the father-image of classical Roman law. God-Father is clothed with infinite power because his care, his sollicitude, his responsibility for every living thing are infinite. Tertullian, the Roman lawyer, sees the invocation, "Our Father," as teaching by the very term the "Son" (Jn. 10:30) and the "Mother," the church: the Lord's Prayer is the prayer of the baptized whom the church has reborn and who have joined God's family. The infinite *distance* rather than the Lactantian connection between the infinite deity of God and the notion of "Father" in the address is keenly felt by many (Cyprian; Gregory of Nyssa; Chrysostom). Some point to the responsibility which this address imposes on those who utter it lest, by their lives, they prove unworthy of the privilege of childhood. Wherever this privilege of childhood is stressed, however, it is clear that biblical adoption-passages guide the argument, first and foremost among them Jn. 1:11-12: "He came to what was his own, and his own people did not accept him. But to all who received him, who believed in his name, he gave power to become children of God."

In this case, however, the first part of the quotation, v. 11, also fueled the ubiquitous argument of supercession. Origen noted that, while God is called the "father" of Israel in the Old Testament, he is never invoked as such. To Moses, another "name" for God was revealed (Ex. 3:14); only Christ opened up the possibility of addressing God as "Father."[43] In rejecting the Son, the Jews rejected the Father. Is. 1:2-4 or 2-9 was often quoted for the rejection of God by the Jewish nation and its consequences, and Tertullian adduced Jn. 8:44 to radicalize the judgment: Not God, the devil is now their father.

b. Tertullian and Cyprian already made a distinction between the first three petitions and the last four. The first three, they explained, concern "heavenly" things, the other four "earthly" ones. Augustine was somewhat

[42] A. Wlosok, "Vater und Vatervorstellungen in der römischen Kultur," in *Das Vaterbild im Abendland*, ed. H. Tellenbach (Stuttgart, 1976), vol. 1, pp. 18-54. Her argument is used in J. Moltmann's discussion of the "Our Father" in an article entitled, "Ich glaube an Gott den Vater: Patriarchalische oder nicht-patriarchalische Rede von Gott?" *Evangelische Theologie* 43 (1983): 397-415.

[43] XXII.1-2; Oulton and Chadwick, *Alexandrian Christianity*, pp. 280-281.

more precise, applying a more differentiated eschatology: "The first three petitions refer to things which will find their fulfillment in eternity only, even though they begin here on earth. . . . The other four, it seems to me, concern the needs of the present life."[44] Nearly every interpreter notes that the first petitions cannot intend to add anything to that which God already has or is. God is perfect in himself. Biblical cross-references establish this basic assumption. God's name, nothing less than "Being" itself (Ex. 3:14), *is* holy (Is. 6:3; Ex. 20:4; Lev. 19:4); God's kingdom, his rulership *are* realities now (Ps. 22:28; 93:1-2; 103:19; 145:13); God's will *is* done. The interpretation of this latter petition was often guided by Jesus' prayer at Gethsemane (Mt. 26:39, 42 par.) which suggested that the petition aims at the virtue of obedience, most perfectly fulfilled in the martyrs (Tertullian; Cyprian). It is possible that this "obvious" biblical key reenforced the general tendency to internalize and personalize all three initial petitions, including the first: Hallowed be your name—*in us* or *by us*. Chrysostom ethicized this phrase: hallowed by our good works which correspond to God's good name (Mt. 5:16). If such works are lacking, God's name is defamed, "blasphemed" (Origen; Gregory of Nyssa; Peter Chrysologus, citing Rom. 2:24).

c. "Your kingdom come"—not that God's eternal rule could be in doubt; rather, we pray that this rule may prevail "*in us* or *for us*," in our personal lives. Origen referred to Lk. 17:20 and Jn. 14:23 for the inwardness of the kingdom; Ambrose to Jn. 19:37. The eschatological dimension is present here (as in some other writers) through the image of the spiritual warfare: We pray for God's rule of knowledge and wisdom to grow in us against the tyranny of the ruler of this world, the devil (Gal. 1:4; Rom. 6:12). Quite clearly, however, the accent on the inward kingdom could be tempered or even overshadowed by apocalyptic kingdom-passages, especially Mt. 25:34 ("Then the king will say . . . Come you blessed . . . inherit the kingdom"): We pray for the final revelation of God's rule "soon" (Tertullian), "at the end" (Cyprian), in the resurrection (Chrysostom).

d. "Your will be done on earth as in heaven." The internalization of the petition (". . . be done in us, by us") forced a metaphorical understanding of "heaven and earth." Closest to the primary meaning of the text was the phrase, "among angels and humans." The most frequent interpretation, however, was the anthropological division of flesh and spirit: We pray that not only our spirit but also the flesh may be brought into obedience to God. Cyprian thought of "unbelievers" and "saints": We pray that unbelievers

---

[44] *Sermon on the Mount* II.10.36-37; cf. Jepsen, p. 124; *Sermon* 58.12; NPNF 6, p. 288.

too may be led to do the will of God. In this case, he argued, the petition also fulfills Jesus' injunction to pray for (= love) one's enemies. Augustine added a fourth option, Christ and the church, probably thinking of Eph. 5:32. The accent was on fullness, unity, often the final, eschatological oneness of all things. Origen referred to 1 Cor. 15:28 ("God all in all") and extended the phrase to the entire group of the three petitions, while Chrysostom stressed the implied call for action in the present: "Even before we reach heaven, we should turn the earth into heaven and live here in such a way as if we were there already" (XIX.5).

e. The most extensive commentary was normally reserved for the fourth petition: "Give us today our daily bread."[45] According to Tertullian, it opens the second part of the Prayer which concerns this present life. Thus, the "simple" meaning of the bread as food for bodily sustenance was considered as one option by several writers. Tertullian already referred to Mt. 6:33 in this connection: ". . . all these things will be yours as well." Where the "simple" meaning was seriously discussed, however, "daily" and "today" suggested an important qualification: Christians should pray for no more than a modest diet, enough for the immediate needs of the day but nothing more—no riches, no luxuries (Gregory of Nyssa; Chrysostom). The context, Mt. 6:25-34, clearly enforced this admonition: "Do not worry about tomorrow." Cyprian cited Daniel in the lions' den, Elijah and the raven, as well as Lk. 12:20-21 ("you fool, this very night . . .") as examples of God's care in daily needs. He added a diatribe against the dangers of wealth, quoting 1 Tim. 6:6-10 which is also cited by other writers, e.g., Chrysostom.

Mt. 6:33 with its call to give priority to the kingdom over "all these things" suggested the preference for a "spiritual" meaning of the petition. Since Tertullian, Cyprian, and Origen it was indeed the dominant interpretation. The biblical key here was John 6, especially 6:35 and 6:45-51, where Jesus identified himself as the "Bread of Life." Bread equals Jesus—several writers emphasized this general spiritual meaning: We pray for the nourishing presence of Christ in our life, the presence of the Word (Tertullian, Cyprian, Origen), which includes the "life-giving precepts of God" (Augustine). Augustine took care to note that the petition mentions bread only, not drink, as the spiritual food: The reason is that we can absorb bread only after breaking and chewing it. In the same way, "Scripture feeds the soul

---

[45] See W. Dürig, "Die Deutung der Brotbitte des Vaterunsers bei den lateinischen Vätern bis Hieronymus," *Liturgisches Jahrbuch* 18 (1968): 77-86; "Die Exegese der vierten Vaterunser-Bitte bei Augustinus," ibid., 22 (1972): 49-61.

by being opened up and studied."[46] Tertullian already quoted Mt. 26:26 along with John 6: "This is my body." With this combination the eucharistic interpretation was always close at hand. Cyprian unfolded it broadly. It is present, though not conspicuous, even in Origen, Gregory of Nyssa, and the other Eastern Fathers.

Western writers since Ambrose regularly appended an argument for daily communion, polemicizing against the supposed custom in the East to commune less frequently. Scholars are still unable to find much substantiation for this assertion.[47] The biblical support for the polemic is drawn from Job 1:5, Job's daily sacrifice for his children (Ambrose, Augustine) even though the argument seems to be triggered by the Old Latin translation of *epiousion* as *cottidianum*, daily, which may be indebted to the Lukan equivalent for *sēmeron*, today, which is *kath' hēmeran*.

The philological problem of the hapax legomenon *epiousios* was widely recognized. Origen discusses at length the two possible derivations of the word: It may be derived from *ousia*, substance, in which case it means the bread "which is best adapted to the reasonable nature and akin to it in its very substance," i.e., the *logos* of God. It may also be derived from *epienai*, in which case it refers to the "bread appropriate to the coming age which we ask God to give us by anticipation now." Origen regarded the first option as "better," probably because of the connection with John 6.[48] Many authors followed him in this preference (Gregory of Nyssa, Cyril of Jerusalem, Cassian, even Ambrose—despite his Bible's Latin translation in the temporal sense only).

Jerome enriched the philological discussion.[49] Following Origen, he translated *epiousios* as *supersubstantialis*, but tried to bolster this meaning by referring to the Hebrew equivalent *sogolla* (*segullah*) for the similar term *periousios* in Ex. 19:5; Deut. 7:6; 14:2, etc., rendered as *exairetos*, chosen, excellent, special, by Symmachus. In passing, he also referred to the Aramaic equivalent *mahar* in the fourth petition according to the Gospel of the Nazarenes which he translated as *crastinus*, "for tomorrow," "future," echoing Origen's second option.

Origen also discussed the term *sēmeron*, today, in a lengthy discourse— one of the famous passages where he developed his notion of sequential eons

[46] *Sermon on the Mount* II.10.37; cf. Jepsen, p. 175.

[47] B. Botte, *Ambroise de Milan: Des sacrements des mystères*, Sources chrétiennes, 25 (Paris: Les Éditions du Cerf, 1949), p. 19.

[48] XXVII.7-9, 13; Oulton and Chadwick, *Alexandrian Christianity*, pp. 298-300, 302.

[49] *Commentary on Matthew*, I, on Mt. 6:11; CCL 77, p. 37.

which would lead to a final *apokatastasis pantōn*; "I know not how," he added.[50] For him, *sēmeron* refers to this present eon in the form of "one day at a time and every day." In a similar way, Augustine saw "today" as a reference to our present, earthly realm where there still is "time" (Heb. 3:13, "as long as it is called today"), while Ambrose pointed to Heb. 13:8 in order to coordinate "daily" and "today." Where the simple, material interpretation of the bread prevailed, "today" meant "only today": "Since you do not know whether you will be alive the next day, why do you worry about it?" (Chrysostom).

f. The Lukan parallel strongly suggested the identity of "debts" and "sins" in the fifth petition. While acknowledging this conclusion from the parallel evidence, Origen tried to develop the notion of debt as the basis for the apparent reciprocity in the petition: We owe many debts to many people, and many people owe us specific debts.[51] Origen seems to argue for recognizing the net of mutual obligations and for a more lenient attitude toward others as the rational way of dealing with each other in society. Luke's wording of the reciprocity clause ("for we ourselves forgive everyone who is indebted to us") seems to guide this interpretation, but also Jesus' parable of the unmerciful servant in Mt. 18:21-35, the most important cross-reference in the interpretation of this petition. This parable kept the primary financial context of the term "debts" vividly before the eyes of the interpreter. In combination with the strong injunction of Mt. 6:14 ("if you forgive others . . ."), it encouraged most exegetes to emphasize our obligation to forgive as a condition for God's forgiveness of *our* sins. Chrysostom notes that Mt. 6:14, the verse immediately following the Lord's Prayer in Matthew, takes up this one petition only. Apparently it makes a central point: "The beginning therefore is our duty, and in our hands rests our own judgment" (Mt. 7:1-2). Cyril of Jerusalem is even more direct: "It is a contract with God when we pray that he may pardon our sins as we forgive our neighbors their debts." Even Augustine's exegesis seems to stand in this tradition: We must pray for the forgiveness of our sins and must forgive others in order to deserve such forgiveness.[52] According to him, the petition includes no less than four elements: the reminder of our continued sinfulness; of the necessity of baptism; of the need for the prayer of forgiveness for post-baptismal sins; and of the duty to forgive others, if not our enemies, then at least those who ask our forgiveness—a reference to Mt. 18:29.

[50] XXVII.13-16; Oulton and Chadwick, *Alexandrian Christianity*, pp. 302-305.
[51] XXVIII.1-6; ibid., pp. 305-308.
[52] *Sermon* 56.13; NPNF 6, p. 278.

g. For the vast majority of interpreters, the sixth petition could not mean that we pray to be spared temptation altogether. Biblical cross-references were all too clear about the fact that temptation is a constant reality in human life: "Is not all human life a place of temptation on earth?" (Job 7:1 LXX; Origen; Chrysologus). Augustine, who regarded temptation as an important ingredient, even a potential blessing (Jas. 1:12) in the pilgrimage of this life, distinguished the temptations experienced by Joseph, Susanna, Job, Peter, the disciples (Lk. 22:46, Tertullian), from those of Cain and Judas.[53] This indicates the general direction in which the interpretations move: We pray that we may stand firm, not be overcome by temptation. Jas. 1:13-14 seemed to establish that God does not tempt; the devil does, although with divine permission (Tertullian; Cyprian). Cyprian made the necessary change in the wording of the petition itself: "Do not allow us to be led into temptation" (also Ambrose). God may allow such temptations as tests for his saints in order to prove their faith and virtues (Abraham: Gen. 22:1; Job; Paul: 2 Cor. 4:7-9, 12:8-10; Jesus himself). For Origen, 1 Cor. 10:13 marks the limits of our temptations, and while it is "impossible" not to be tempted, it is possible not to succumb to them like Jesus who "looked through the lattice" of our imprisonment and says to our soul: "Arise, my love, . . . and come away" (Song 2:9-10).[54]

h. In line with the interpretation of the sixth petition, most writers read "apo tou ponērou" in the seventh petition as a masculine noun: "deliver us from the evil one," the devil. Again, Origen could invoke the image of the valiant fight of the Christian saint, Job being the prime example as he proved the devil a liar. Chrysostom noted that the petition uses the singular, not the plural (ponērōn); the devil is the cause of all evil, not by nature, but as the epitome of the misuse of free will and malice against the human race. Augustine sees the depth of this last petition in its ability to sum up in one phrase the entire meaning of prayer as our call for deliverance from the depth of human experience:

> When we say 'Deliver us from evil,' we admonish ourselves to consider that we are not yet enjoying that bliss in which we will experience no evil. This last petition is so comprehensive that Christians, whatever affliction they may experience, can give words to their inward groans and vent to their tears. They may begin with this petition, go on with it, and with it conclude all prayer.[55]

[53] Sermon on the Mount II.9.30-32; Jepsen, pp. 118-120.
[54] XXIX.9; Oulton and Chadwick, Alexandrian Christianity, p. 314.
[55] Letter 130.XI.21; NPNF 1, p. 466.

VIII

In his entire exegesis of the Lord's Prayer, Augustine demonstrates in a powerful way how strongly the vision of a unified biblical witness really governs all the details of the interpretation. For him, every line of the language of Scripture in all its limitation is full of mysteries which can and should be sought out. It is well known how deep an interest he had in biblical numerology. Finding significant numbers and numerical relations in Scripture meant lifting its ambiguous language into a realm of much less ambiguity, a language closer to the reality of creation, and thus of the creator. The structure of Jesus' entire Sermon on the Mount, he suggested, is governed by the seven makarisms (if one counts the eighth as a "repetition" of the first). They correspond to the seven gifts of the Spirit (Is. 11:2-3).[56] Augustine's interpretation of the Lord's Prayer comes in the exposition of the sixth makarism ("blessed are the pure in heart, for they will see God"), its own seven petitions (three, the number of God's world, plus four, the number of our world) marvelously coordinated with the seven makarisms. What they teach is the sevenfold ascent to God, the *perfectus vitae Christi modus*, which leads us to our final goal with the help of the Spirit.

If we take seriously the hermeneutical presuppositions of this form of exegesis which is shared by all patristic writers, it becomes clear that this paper could not present a developmental picture of the patristic interpretation of the Lord's Prayer. Even if the varieties, the interdependencies, and the nuances could be spelled out more fully in each case, they would reflect an enrichment of the recognized store of applicable biblical cross-references, not a change in scope. *Scriptura sui ipsius interpres*: scripture is its own interpreter. Underlying all the personal theological accents and catechetical or liturgical agendas which are present in the writings of our authors, this, it seems to me, is the "principle" of the patristic exegesis of the Lord's Prayer.

[56] *Sermon on the Mount*, I.3.10-4.11; Jepsen, pp. 16-20.

John Calvin's Teaching on the Lord's Prayer

by ELSIE ANNE McKEE

THE SIXTEENTH-CENTURY Reformation is remembered as a time of renewal in the worship, teaching, and life of the Christian church. It is
natural, then, that the Lord's Prayer was a subject of considerable importance, and in fact many expositions of the Lord's Prayer were produced by
Christians of different languages and varied confessions.

Vernacular explanations of the Lord's Prayer were not really new, though
it was unusual for people to begin to pray this special prayer regularly in
their own language.[1] In the sixteenth century even lay people, or others with
no formal pastoral charge, were eager to expound the Lord's Prayer for their
friends. One may think of the devout and lively Katharina Schütz Zell of
Strasbourg, who wrote out a clear and simple explanation of the Lord's
Prayer at the request of some acquaintances who appealed for her help in
understanding how to live according to God's will.[2] Or the mystical Span-
iard Juan de Valdés, whose *Commentary on Matthew*, and many other
works, were written for a circle of Italian evangelicals gathered around the
Duchess Guilia Gonzaga.[3]

---

[1] For example, an explanation of the Lord's Prayer was one common element of the popular late medieval vernacular preaching service called "prône." Individually, pious medieval
parents taught their children to recite the Lord's Prayer in Latin, but many did not really
understand this. In early Protestant Geneva, many discipline cases were concerned with the
simple people's ignorance of basics of the faith. Often elderly people, especially women, were
unable to explain the meaning of the Prayer, even when they knew it in Latin; the Consistory
frequently required such people to learn the Prayer in their own language before they would
be (re)admitted to the Lord's Supper. See R. M. Kingdon, "How the Consistory Helped to
Convert Geneva to Calvinism," presented at the Sixteenth Century Studies Conference, October 1988.

[2] Katharina Schütz Zell, *Den Psalmen miserere . . .* , 1558, A7v-A8r, E4v-J3r. She says she
wrote this explanation in 1532 for two women of the city of Speyer. I am preparing a full
study of Katharine Schütz Zell; at this time there exists no translation, although short ex-
cerpts are quoted in some secondary sources. Zell also explains the Lord's Prayer briefly in
the impromptu sermon she preached at her husband's funeral in January 1548. (Here and in
all following notes, in writings in which the Lord's Prayer is only a part, the page numbers
refer only to the material on the Prayer itself.)

[3] Juan de Valdés, *Lo Evangelio di San Matteo*, ed. C. Ossola, text A. M. Cavallarin (Roma:
Bulzoni, 1985), pp. 196-200. [*San Matteo*] Compare the earlier version of the Lord's Prayer in

Among the most influential of all writers was Martin Luther. The great German reformer produced a number of texts explaining the Lord's Prayer. The two earliest of these, *The German Explanation of the Lord's Prayer for Simple Laity*, published in 1519, and the *Little Prayer Book* of 1522, were first written in German. They were soon translated into Latin and vernaculars such as French, thus reaching ever wider audiences. In 1529 Luther produced his *Larger Catechism*, while a new and somewhat different form of the *Little Prayer Book* appeared as the Smaller Catechism. Both of these texts, including expositions of the Lord's Prayer, were also immediately available in Latin.[4]

To attempt to treat here all the writings on the Lord's Prayer published in the Protestant Reformation would be to court incoherence or superficiality, if not disaster, so the focus of this presentation is restricted to John Calvin's teaching on the Prayer. However, it is necessary to place Calvin's work in historical context in two ways. First, Calvin was a generation younger than Luther, and thus it is appropriate to compare and contrast Calvin's thought with that of some of his most important predecessors, specifically the humanist Erasmus, and the Protestants Martin Luther and Martin Bucer. (The church fathers Calvin used are also mentioned, but not considered in depth.) Secondly, Calvin himself learned and grew throughout his busy life, from his conversion until his death. It is very interesting to see the development of his thought over time, in order to appreciate the nuances and richness of what he says about the Lord's Prayer.[5]

These two facts: the historical context, and the development of Calvin's own thought, have shaped the method and order followed in this study. The first point is a brief sketch of the relationship between Calvin's thought and some of the major expositions of the Lord's Prayer which he knew. Then comes a short summary of the different stages of development in Calvin's doctrine, and an outline of the setting of Calvin's teaching on the Lord's Prayer in his wider general discussion of prayer. This is followed by a few

---

Valdés' *Dialogue on Christian Doctrine* [January 1529], ed. J. C. Nieto, in *Valdés' Two Catechisms* (Coronado Press, 1981), pp. 132-140. [*Dialogue*]

[4] *D. Martin Luthers Werke* (Weimar: Hermann Bohlau, 1883-). "Auslegung deutsch des Vaterunsers für einfältigen Laien," WA 2, pp. 80-130 (Latin 1520). "Betbüchlein," WA 10:2, pp. 395-407 (first Latin 1525); in 1529 there appeared a revised Latin edition entitled *Enchiridion piarum precationum* (or "Der Kleine Katechismus"), WA 30:1, pp. 298-309. "Deutsch Katechismus," WA 30:1, pp. 193-211 (Latin 1529). See below, n. 46, for the question of changes in 1529.

[5] Calvin is a "second-generation reformer," but not a second-generation Protestant. This is important to remember in studying the development of Calvin's thought, since the latter reflects changes which in some ways parallel those of "first-generation reformers."

words about the paradigmatic role of the Lord's Prayer as model for all right prayer, and a note on Calvin's understanding of the structure of the Prayer. The central portion of the presentation is a more detailed exposition of each part of the Lord's Prayer, which combines a kind of historical approach with a summary of Calvin's mature teaching.

I. Sources and Development of Calvin's Thought

Sources. Martin Luther's explanations of the Lord's Prayer were the most important in the early Reformation, and continued to have an enormous influence, but in fact they were apparently not the most critical for John Calvin. That honor goes to Martin Bucer, the leader of the Reformation in Strasbourg and for several years Calvin's elder colleague.[6] Naturally, patristic exegetes such as John Chrysostom were also important influences in Calvin's theological treatment of the Lord's Prayer.

Calvin certainly knew and read Luther's works on the Lord's Prayer which were available in Latin. There are a number of resemblances between Calvin's thought and that of Luther, but the different emphases of the two writers are also notable. Perhaps the most important similarity between Luther and Calvin lies not in the texts themselves but in the fact that both men repeatedly made vernacular explanations of the Lord's Prayer for ordinary Christians. This was a common Protestant activity, but Luther and Calvin seem to have been unusually prolific and influential.

Martin Bucer's discussion of the Lord's Prayer in his commentary on the *Harmony of the (Synoptic) Gospels*, first published in 1527, is clearly very closely related to that of Calvin. Calvin follows Bucer in several important ways, most notably in the petition on daily bread, where both Bucer and Calvin adopt the interpretation of John Chrysostom's homilies on Matthew.[7]

Calvin is no mere follower, however, and never simply a copyist. His treatment of the Lord's Prayer, particularly in later years, is characterized by independent judgment and especially by a clarity and brevity, coherence

---

[6] See A. Ganoczy, *Le jeune Calvin* (Wiesbaden: Steiner, 1966), pp. 171-175. Also, below at nn. 46, 68-69.

[7] Bucer, *Enarrationes Perpetuae in Sacra Quatuor Evangelia* (Argentorati apud Georgium Ulricherum Andlanum, 1530), tome 1, f62r-67v for Mt. 6:1-13. [*Enarrationes*] I have consulted both the 1527 and the 1530 editions, but here use the pagination of 1530, since there is an English translation of this edition. (See appendix in *Calvin. Institutes of the Christian Religion* (1536 Edition), trans. F. L. Battles [Grand Rapids: Wm. B. Eerdmans, 1975], pp. 343-362. [*Institutes 1536*] This translation is for the most part readable, but in places it is confusing and inept.) Not all similarities between Bucer and Calvin will be noted, but for some of the most important, see below at nn. 22-23, 47-49, 68-69. For Chrysostom, see "Homiliae in Matthaeum," in *Patrilogiae Graecae*, ed. J. P. Migne (Paris, 1862), vol. 57, no. 19, col. 273-286. [MPG]

and order, which are hallmarks of his thought generally. For example, although Calvin read Erasmus on the Lord's Prayer, he frankly criticizes the great humanist's interpretation on particular points, such as the relationship of God to mundane matters like physical nourishment. As often in exegetical matters, the works of John Chrysostom were especially important to Calvin as to Bucer, but Calvin does not hesitate to disagree politely with both of his mentors on some issues such as the identity of the evil from which we pray to be delivered.[8]

Development, 1536-1559. When one examines Calvin's teaching on the Lord's Prayer, it quickly becomes evident that there is not just one locus in which to find it. The 1559 *Institutes of the Christian Religion* is the natural place to look, and the single fullest form, but to restrict one's view to that final statement is to miss the pleasure of watching a child mature.

The earliest exposition of the Lord's Prayer is found in the first edition of the *Institutes*, in 1536. This text serves as the basis for all the later developments, and most of Calvin's ideas are sketched or at least adumbrated here. There is, however, a real development over the years. Calvin's first Catechism of 1537 includes a short exposition of the Lord's Prayer in French, which is almost a translation of portions of the 1536 *Institutes*.[9] A certain number of additions are made in the 1539 *Institutes*; these can be more easily traced in the first French translation of 1541, since the 1539 *Institutes* has not been easily available.[10] Some of the 1539 additions fill out the discussion by naming and refuting opposing views which the first edition had passed over in silence.

---

[8] Bucer follows Chrysostom in identifying evil as the devil (Bucer, *Enarrationes*, f67v, Eng. p. 361; Chrysostom, MPG 57:282). Calvin (like Erasmus) calmly says that it may be either Satan or sin, but it does not matter which we choose since it means about the same thing. (Added in 1539; see *Jean Calvin: Institution de la Religion Chretienne*, ed. J. Pannier [Paris: Sociéte des Belles Lettres, 1936-39], pp. 189-190. [*Institution 1541*]) For Erasmus' comment, see *Opera Omnia* (Lugduni Batavorum: Petri Vander Aa, 1703-06), *Novum Testamentum*, vol. 6, col. 35.

[9] *Christianae Religionis Institutio 1536*, in *Johannis Calvini Opera Selecta*, ed. P. Barth et al. (Monachii in Aedibus: Chr. Kaiser, 1926-52), vol. 1. [*Opera Selecta* = OS and *Institutes 1536*] In *Institutes 1536*, chap. 3 concerns prayer; hereafter the chapter number will be omitted as being understood. Chapter on prayer is OS 1:96-117. "Instruction et Confession de Foy" (Catechism 1537), OS 1:405-410. In this early prose catechism Calvin does not comment on the final doxology.

[10] See *Institution 1541*, vol. 3, chap. 9. Hereafter volume and chapter will be omitted as being understood. Pannier marks the 1539 and (rare) 1541 additions, but he does not always indicate where the 1536 text has been slightly modified, so for the purpose of studying Calvin's development this edition should be used with some caution. (There are also some differences between the Latin and French *Institutes* throughout, but these are not a concern of the present study.) See R. F. Wevers, *Institutes of the Christian Religion of John Calvin, 1539: Text and Concordance* (Grand Rapids: Meeter Center, 1988). This is the first modern edition.

In 1542, two more versions of the Lord's Prayer appeared, each different from the *Institutes* in style though similar in orientation. Both of these, like the first catechism, were written directly in French. One of these was Calvin's liturgy, *La Forme des Prières*. The Sunday service includes a rather lengthy paraphrase of the Lord's Prayer as the final part of the prayer of intercession after the sermon.[11] Here one sees characteristic expressions of Calvin's understanding of the Lord's Prayer in the way he rephrases the various petitions. For example, in regard to forgiving others, Calvin leads the congregation to pray not only that they may cease to be angry with those who have harmed them, but also that they may seek good relationships with these enemies.

The Genevan Catechism of 1542 is considerably fuller than its 1537 predecessor, but it adds little to the content of the Lord's Prayer as found in the 1539 *Institutes*. (One of those rare additions will be noted below.) Perhaps the most significant feature of this portion of the catechism is the clarity with which this little classic reveals the place of prayer in Calvin's larger theology.[12]

There are no additions to the teaching on the Lord's Prayer in the next revisions of the *Institutes* published in 1543 and 1550, but in his commentary on the *Harmony of the (Synoptic) Gospels* in 1555,[13] Calvin significantly develops his teaching, and these alterations are then carried over into the final edition of the *Institutes* in 1559.[14] In this period Calvin enriches his basic exposition of the Lord's Prayer with a number of new nuances; he also adds some very interesting comments relating different petitions of the prayer and linking them with other parts of his theology.[15] Calvin's last discussions

11 "La Forme des Prières," OS 2:(22)23-24. English translation in B. Thompson, *Liturgies of the Western Church* (Cleveland: World Publishing Co, 1961 [1975]), pp. 201-202.

12 "Le Catéchisme de Genève," *Iohannis Calvini Opera Quae Supersunt Omnia*, ed. G. Baum, E. Cunitz, and E. Reuss (Brunsvigae: Schwetschke et Filium, 1863-1900), vol. 6, pp. 91-106. [*Opera Calvini* = OC] French 1542 and Latin 1545 are in parallel columns; Latin is also in OS 2:118-127. English in *Calvin: Theological Treatises*, ed. J. K. S. Reid (Philadelphia: Westminster, 1954), pp. 122-129.

13 *Harmonia ex tribus Evangelistis composita . . .*, OC 45:195-203. English: *A Harmony of the Gospels: Matthew, Mark and Luke*, trans. A. W. Morrison, ed. D. W. Torrance and T. F. Torrance (Grand Rapids: Wm. B. Eerdmans, 1980), vol. 2, pp. 204-213. [*Harmony*] See the brief comment on the relationship of Matthew to Luke, in n. 22. At various points Calvin refers to Luke's words, e.g., comparing Matthew's "debts" with Luke's "sins," but generally he follows Matthew because the latter "brings all the chief points of the the the teaching together, that readers may have a better perspective over the whole in an unbroken sequence." See *Harmony*, OC 45:194, 201, Eng. pp. 204-205, 212.

14 *Institutes 1559* 3.20.34-47. *Institutio Christianae Religionis 1559*, OS 4:344-365. English: *Calvin: Institutes of the Christian Religion*, ed. J. T. McNeill, trans. F. L. Battles (Philadelphia: Westminster, 1960), vol. 2, pp. 897-916. [*Institutes 1559* for Latin and English.]

15 See below, at nn. 32, 52.

of the Lord's Prayer, in his homilies on the synoptic gospels, preached in the early 1560's, are unhappily not extant, since the stenographer who was recording the sermons died in 1562, while Calvin was working through the fifth chapter of Matthew.[16]

Context: Prayer, the Chief Exercise of Devotion. Calvin, like many others, locates his treatment of the Lord's Prayer in the setting of a general consideration of Christian prayer. This order is biblical as well as logical. Matthew was the dominant voice in the synoptics in the sixteenth century, and in Matthew, prior to giving them the particular form known as the Lord's Prayer, Jesus teaches his disciples how to pray, and specifically says they are not to do as the Pharisees.

Thus, before beginning to explain the Lord's Prayer, Calvin discusses the manner in which one should pray. Like many other reformers, Calvin emphasizes the importance of inward and spiritual prayer. Fundamentally, prayer is a matter of the heart and spirit, although the tongue may have a part, especially in corporate praise. Calvin objects strongly to external show; prayer is not heard because it is wordy, and it is not to be done to impress other people. Most importantly, no one ever prays rightly without faith in God and an awareness of personal sinfulness. Prayer begins with acknowledging our unworthiness and need, and affirming trust in God's mercy as the sole and sufficient source of hope. It is wrong, indeed fatal, to rely on one's own merits or those of any other person, no matter how good; Calvin, like others, attacks the invocation of the (dead) saints. The right attitude is to put all trust in God's mercy and in Christ's intercession, and none in oneself.[17]

The instruction to pray in secret leads to a consideration of where and when one should pray. Calvin affirms that both individual and corporate prayer are commanded, but over time the balance between the two shifts. In 1536 the emphasis is largely non-institutional, but by 1539 there are signs of change, as Calvin moves towards his fully developed ecclesiology. That development is a topic for another occasion. Here it is sufficient to say that the Lord's Prayer plays an important role in both private and communal prayer.[18]

[16] See OC 46:iv. The text of the last sermon extant is Mt. 5:11-12/Lk. 6:22-26.

[17] The first example is *Institutes 1536*, OS 1:96-105, Eng. pp. 68-76; similar material throughout, till it reaches full development in *Institutes 1559*, 3.20.1-33, 48-52. (In this section Calvin also discusses why one should pray. I am grateful to Prof. Willis-Watkins for raising this issue in his response to my paper at the Neumann Symposium. Calvin answers primarily by saying that God both commands us to pray, and promises to hear our prayers [cf. esp. 3.20.1-3]. I hope to develop this point further in another context.

[18] See *Institutes 1536*, OS 1:102-104, Eng. pp. 73-75; cf. *Institutes 1559*, 3.20.28-33, Eng.

The Right Rule of Praying. For Calvin, prayer is the chief exercise of piety, the center of worship, and the Lord's Prayer is the perfect rule for right prayer, the specific form which Christ provided to show his disciples for what they should pray. The attitude or manner of prayer is the principal thing, but the way or form is also critically important, and having Christ's own instruction is a very special gift to help us in our weakness and sin. The Lord's Prayer includes all that we should ask; Calvin calls it the pattern or model or rule of right praying.[19]

The Lord's Prayer is our perfect model, but this does not mean that we are constrained to use only its precise words. Calvin himself did not hesitate to paraphrase the text for Sunday worship, to enable the people better to understand what they were asking. He also points out that there are many scriptural prayers inspired by the same Spirit, which use words different from the Lord's Prayer. The point is that these prayers, and all right prayers, must tend to the same end as the Lord's Prayer.[20]

The Divisions of the Lord's Prayer. Traditionally the Lord's Prayer was often divided into a preface or foreword, seven petitions, and frequently a kind of conclusion. Luther and others in the sixteenth century follow Augustine and others in dividing the petitions into seven,[21] but Bucer and Calvin do not. Instead of reading "deliver us from evil" as the seventh request, these two reformers, like Chrysostom, consider this phrase the second part of the sixth petition, which they read as follows: "lead us not into temptation, but deliver us from evil." In reaching this conclusion Calvin is also

---

2:888-897. Below at nn. 29-30 and n. 37. I am presently engaged in a more detailed examination of Calvin's teaching on worship, especially public worship and the relationship between public and private worship.

[19] See esp. *Institutes 1536*, OS 1:104, Eng. p. 75. For examples of various words Calvin uses: *Institutes 1536*, OS 1:104, 107 (*forma, regula, formula, "in tabula," lex*); Catechism 1537, OS 1:405 (*forme, reigle*); Institution 1541, pp. 168-169 (*stile, formulaire, reigle*); Catechism 1542, OC 6:91 (*formulaire*); *Harmony*, OC 45:195 (*regula, lex*). (*Institutes 1559* does not add anything new, but takes over the 1536 text.) There does not appear to be any significant difference in meaning intended, though it is interesting to note that these are contrasted with such words as *ratio* (OS 1:104), which describe the attitude or manner.

[20] *Institutes 1536*, OS 1:115-116, Eng. pp. 84-86; *Institutes 1559*, 3.20.48-49. The Holy Spirit not only inspired the biblical prayers, but (as Calvin adds in 1539) the same Spirit repeatedly suggests to believers (other) prayers which are not the same words as the Lord's Prayer (see 3.20.49). Thus Calvin does not restrict the guiding of the Holy Spirit to the biblically recorded prayers, but it is clear that the same Spirit will always inspire prayers in accord with the pattern Christ gave in the Lord's Prayer. For Calvin's paraphrase, see n. 11.

[21] See Luther's various texts listed in n. 4. Katharina Schütz Zell, Valdés, and Erasmus' *Precatio Dominica* are other examples of seven (see nn. 2-3, 44). One influential patristic source for this division was Augustine (see "Enchiridion 30:115-116" in *Patrologiae Latina*, ed. J. P. Migne [Paris, 1865], vol. 40, p. 285, cited in McNeill-Battles' *Institutes 1559*, 2:898, n. 70). For other church fathers, see K. Froehlich's article on the Lord's Prayer in this volume.

influenced by the discrepancy between Matthew and Luke, since the latter omits "deliver us from evil." Calvin seeks here to harmonize the two gospels, insisting that Luke would not have left out anything of importance.[22]

Another division, which is more important for Bucer and Calvin, is the grouping of the six petitions into two parts, each containing three points. The three petitions of part one are concerned first and foremost with God and what is owed to God; the second set of three petitions is concerned with human needs. Both parts are ultimately concerned with God's glory but both also benefit believers.[23] It is interesting to note that in his gospel harmony commentary in 1555, Calvin explicitly likens the two parts of the Lord's Prayer to the two tables of the law. The first three petitions, like the first table of the law, are concerned with the glory and worship of God. The final three petitions of the prayer, like the second table of the law, deal with matters of human life and common sharing, although their ultimate purpose is still the right service of God.[24]

II. THE LORD'S PRAYER

"OUR FATHER." The first words of the Lord's Prayer are normally understood as a kind of preface or address for the whole prayer. Calvin, like other interpreters, discusses a number of common topics, but he also gives a distinctively Protestant turn to the explanation, and adds particular nuances of his own.[25]

[22] For Bucer, *Enarrationes*, f64r, 67r, Eng. pp. 350, 361. Chrysostom does not actually object to seven, but he treats "lead us not into temptation, but deliver us from evil," as a single point; see MPG 57:282. See Calvin's explanation, *Institutes 1536*, OS 1:104, Eng. p. 75: "The reason why I do not agree with those who distinguish seven headings is that in Luke [Luke 11:2-4] only six are read; obviously he would not have left the prayer in a defective form, so that what has been added in seventh place in Matthew exegetically ought to be referred to the sixth petition." Unlike modern texts, Erasmus' New Testament included "thy will be done," and "deliver us from evil," in Luke 11:2, 4, although in his notes Erasmus gives another version which lacks both phrases. Erasmus, *Opera Omnia, Novum Testamentum*, vol. 6, col. 276. Dr. Irena Backus suggests that the fact that "deliver us from evil" is the only omission on which Erasmus comments probably indicates that this particular omission had gained a special status and required explanation. In his note on "deliver us from evil," Erasmus adds the other variants, as if to complete the discussion, but not as if these were of equal importance. (My thanks to Dr. Backus for this suggestion.)

[23] Bucer, *Enarrationes*, f64r, Eng. pp. 350-351. For Calvin, the earliest example is *Institutes 1536*, OS 1:104-105, Eng. pp. 75-76. There are similarities to this two-fold division among church fathers (see Froehlich), but Calvin's expression is characteristically his own. Repeatedly the reformer insists that all six requests have as their primary goal the glory of God, but in fact every part also benefits believers.

[24] *Harmony*, OC 45:195, 198, Eng. pp. 205, 209.

[25] In the following notes, only the first appearance of an idea will be noted. Unless otherwise stated, it may be assumed that the idea, if not always the wording, remains constant until the end. Changes or additions will be noted. In some cases, the formulation here follows

Calvin speaks first of the importance of our calling God "Father." This is possible only through Christ, because it is only in Christ that we have the privilege of becoming children of God, when God puts the Holy Spirit in our hearts to enable us to trust and to cry "Abba." Without Christ as mediator, there is no possibility of coming to God.[26] However, Christ is the only intercessor we need, and then we, though sinners, may approach God our Father directly; indeed, we must do so, acting in the faith and trust which God's goodness to us inspires. Calvin says that the privilege of calling God "Father" frees us from fears (*diffidentia*). We must not make even our sinfulness an excuse for avoiding God, because if we seek help anywhere else than in our Father, we are in fact accusing God of cruelty or poverty, as if our Father did not love us or have the power to meet our needs. God welcomes repentant sons and daughters just as the father in the parable welcomed his prodigal son.[27]

The interpretation of God's being "in heaven" is hinted in this discussion of God as Father. First, "heaven" means God's glory; it is not a place but evidence of God's majesty and power. However, this power is for our assurance, because it signifies that God can provide for those who believe. The appeal to "the Father" expresses our access and God's goodness and love; the reference to "heaven" confirms God's ability to care for those who trust God's mercy in Christ. Calling on God as our "Father in heaven" not only engenders trust but also is a guard against the temptation to idolatry, to keep us from being drawn away to false gods.[28]

One of the interesting parts of this preface is the way that Calvin treats the word "our." It is common for interpreters to point out that this plural is important, as a sign that no one should claim God as his or her Father alone, to the exclusion of others. Calvin's formulation of this traditional idea is, however, somewhat distinctive. First he points out that this word "our" is an indication of the kind of brotherly love which we ought to feel for each other, as common children of such a father.

The prayer of the Christian man ought then to be conformed to this rule in order that it may be in common and embrace all who are his

that of the commentary, even when the idea is present in the earlier *Institutes*; that fact is also noted.

[26] *Institutes 1536*, OS 1:105-106, Eng. p. 76. *et passim*. The reference to the Holy Spirit is added in 1559 (*Institutes 1559*, 3.20.37, OS 4:347-348, Eng. 2:900-901).

[27] See esp. *Institutes 1536*, OS 1:105-106, Eng. pp. 76-77.

[28] *Institutes 1536*, OS 1:108, Eng. p. 78, gives the general sense but the fullness is found in *Harmony*, OC 45:195-196, Eng. p. 206. The final sentence (vs. idolatry) is added in *Institutes 1559*, 3.20.40, OS 4:350, Eng. 2:903.

brothers in Christ, not only those whom he at present sees and recognizes as such but all men who dwell on earth. For what the Lord has determined concerning them is beyond our knowing, except that we ought to wish and hope the best for them. Yet we ought to be drawn with a special affection to those, above others, of the household of faith.[29]

Note that Calvin includes all people who dwell on earth—unexpected in someone who is usually identified primarily with predestination!

The emphasis on "our" makes prayers common, because the object is the shared good of all. We may pray for ourselves and particular individuals, but only if we keep the community always in mind and never turn away from it. Calvin draws a comparison between prayer and almsgiving. Both are commands of God by which we serve others, but almsgiving is more restricted because we can help only those we can see.[30] In the final edition of the *Institutes*, Calvin adds a further note. According to Paul's teaching, "strife shuts the gate to prayers," and thus Christians should "offer their petitions in common with one accord."[31]

As Calvin explains it, the opening words of the Lord's Prayer teach believers that they must approach God with trust, through Christ. Even though they are sinners, believers will find God a loving Father both willing to save them, and powerful enough to do so, because Christ mediates for them and the Holy Spirit witnesses that they are the adopted children of God. Believers do not pray for themselves alone, however; all their prayers should look to the common good of all God's children, near and far, known and unknown.

The First Three Petitions. The first three petitions of the Lord's Prayer are directed to God. In each discussion Calvin treats the points in order, but there are a number of changes over time, between the 1530's and the 1550's, particularly in the second petition. These changes are primarily substitutions which do not alter the basic meaning. As Calvin makes explicit in 1555, "there is a great affinity and likeness [among the first three petitions]. The hallowing of God's Name is always attached to His reign, and the chief feature of His reign is to be acknowledged in the doing of His will." It is not superfluous for Christ to distinguish the three points, however, since we are so cold and apathetic that we need the triple list.[32]

[29] *Institutes 1536*, OS 1:107, Eng. p. 77.
[30] *Institutes 1536*, OS 1:107, Eng. p. 78.
[31] *Institutes 1559*, 3.20.39; OS 4:349, Eng. 2:902.
[32] *Harmony*, OC 45:196, Eng. pp. 206-207.

"HALLOWED BE THY NAME." To hallow God's name is to accord God the honor which is owed to God and not to obscure God's glory in any way. God's holiness is, in itself, always secure, but it can be profaned and obscured by human ingratitude and irreverence.[33] Calvin includes thanksgiving here; we hallow God's name by acknowledging and praising God as is fitting, in short, by worshiping God rightly.

"THY KINGDOM COME." Over time, there is a significant shift of emphasis, though not substance, in Calvin's explanation of the second petition. The first editions of the *Institutes* appear to give somewhat more attention to the invisible church, while in the later writings there is a slightly more institutional orientation.

In Calvin's earliest descriptions of the second petition, he explains that God's kingdom is manifest in two ways: in the Holy Spirit ruling and acting in believers to make God's goodness and mercy known, and in the judgment of the wicked. We pray for God to add new believers and to fill them with gifts so that God's light and truth may shine out, and Satan may be overcome.[34] In 1539, Calvin adds more biblical material to explain what Christ means by "the kingdom of God" which is fundamentally within us. Sometimes "the kingdom of heaven" signifies the church where Christ reigns, sometimes it is the preaching of the gospel, the means by which Christ's reign is established.[35]

In the 1550's, Calvin greatly reworked his discussion of the second petition of the Lord's Prayer. The earlier explanation is largely replaced, although much of 1559 is simply a recasting of 1536-1539.[36] However, one remark on the coming of the kingdom illustrates the shift toward a more institutional focus in Calvin's ecclesiology. The reference to "new believers" in 1536 is replaced here by "churches" and there is a concern for right order.

> We must daily desire that God gather churches unto himself from all parts of the earth; that he spread and increase them in number; that he adorn them with gifts; that he establish a lawful order among them; on the other hand, that he cast down all enemies of pure teaching and religion; that he scatter their counsels and crush their efforts.[37]

[33] *Institutes 1536*, OS 1:108, Eng. pp. 78-79. See *Harmony*, OC 45:196, Eng. p. 207. Substitutions of the 1550's do not significantly change the meaning, although some points (e.g., thanksgiving) are expressed less fully.

[34] *Institutes 1536*, OS 1:109, Eng. p. 79.

[35] *Institution 1541*, p. 179.

[36] *Institutes 1559*, 3.20.42; OS 4:352, Eng. 2:905.

[37] *Institutes 1559*, 3.20.42; OS 4:353, Eng. 2:905.

The commentary expresses clearly the means and the goal of the coming of God's kingdom, giving particular attention to the combination of the Spirit and the Word.[38]

There is an eschatological note in Calvin's discussion of the coming of God's kingdom, but this reference to the fulfilment of Christ's rule is typically moderate. When we pray each day "thy kingdom come," we are asking that God's reign may increase daily and at last be perfected in the revelation of the judgment day when Satan will be finally defeated.[39]

"THY WILL BE DONE." The interpretation of the third petition is similar to that of the second. We ask God to answer our prayers not as we wish but as God foresees is best. We pray not only that what is opposed to God's will may not be done, but also that God may create us afresh to desire what is in accord with that divine will.[40]

In the later writings, both commentary and the 1559 *Institutes*, Calvin adds an explanatory word about a problem in speaking of the will of God. In itself, God's will is one and simple, but for us and in scripture it appears two-fold: the revealed will of God, and then God's secret judgment, by which all things are ruled, whether they wish to obey or not. In this prayer we are not concerned with God's hidden will, but we are taught to ask that all may obey willingly, "that all creatures may yield to [God], in quietness and without hostility."[41] Should we pray for something which God says will never happen until the end of the world, that is, the perfect obedience of all creatures? Calvin replies in a pacific and practical manner. It is sufficient for us to witness by our prayer that we hate all which is opposed to the will of God, so that we may be governed by God's will and eagerly offer ourselves to participate in its fulfilment.[42]

The praying of the first part of the Lord's Prayer is a kind of watershed for Calvin. Those who refuse to hallow God's name, or pray for God's kingdom and will, are not to be reckoned children of God. (Note that the word

---

[38] "So the sum of this supplication is that God will illuminate the heart by the light of His Word, bring our hearts to obey His righteousness by the breathing of His Spirit, and restore to order at His will, all that is lying waste upon the earth" (*Harmony*, OC 45:197, Eng. p. 208).

[39] *Institutes 1536*, OS 1:109, Eng. p. 79. The formulation alters in the 1550's but without significant change, though there is some sense of incremental increase in the kingdom in both the commentary and the *Institutes*. See *Harmony*, OC 45:197-198, Eng. p. 208; *Institutes 1559*, 3.20.42, OS 4:353, Eng. 2:906.

[40] *Institutes 1536*, OS 1:109-110, Eng. pp. 79-80.

[41] *Harmony*, OC 45:198, Eng. p. 208 (quotation); *Institutes 1559*, 3.20.43, OS 4:354, Eng. 2:906. Note the similarities but especially the differences between Calvin and the patristic exegetes here (see Froehlich).

[42] *Harmony*, OC 45:198, Eng. pp. 208-209.

is "reckon," *habendi sunt*; even here Calvin does not speak as if he or the earthly church possesses omniscience regarding the elect and reprobate.) On the other hand, those who truly seek the fulfilment of the first three petitions of the Lord's Prayer testify and profess themselves to be the children of God.[43]

The Second Three Petitions. The second triad of petitions in the Lord's Prayer has reference to human beings' own concerns, though the ultimate purpose is still the glory of God. As in the case of the first part of the prayer, there are developments in Calvin's exposition, here in the form of additions rather than substitutions.

"GIVE US THIS DAY OUR DAILY BREAD." Bucer's and Calvin's discussion of the fourth petition, the request for daily bread, is especially interesting, particularly in contrast with the work of some of the earlier commentators.

According to Erasmus, the "bread" for which we pray is not mere earthly food. In the *Paraphrases*, Erasmus calls the bread "heavenly doctrine," and the longer *Precatio Dominica* is similar.[44] In the *Annotations on the New Testament*, it is less clear precisely what the bread is, but it is also more explicitly described as not being earthly. Erasmus prefers the interpretation "supersubstantial" (beyond natural food), because "in such a heavenly prayer Christ would not speak of that (kind of) bread that even gentiles receive from their parents."[45]

For the early Luther, the principal meaning of "daily bread" is the preaching of the Word, though there are also references to the Lord's Supper and ordinary food. The *Explanation of the Lord's Prayer* in 1519 speaks at some length of the need for good preachers to feed the people spiritual food, especially the Word, but also the sacrament. At the end, physical bread is also mentioned. The first *Little Prayer Book* includes the sacrament with the primary concern of preaching. When Luther published his two cate-

---

[43] *Institutes 1536*, OS 1:110, Eng. p. 80.

[44] Erasmus, *Opera Omnia, Paraphrases*, Mt. 6:11, vol. 7, col. 37: "Ale, Pater, quod genuisti, prospice nobis ne nos deficiat panis ille tuus doctrinae coelestis." See also col. 380 (Luke 11:3). For *Precatio Dominica* see *"A Devout Treatise Upon the Pater Noster* by Desiderius Erasmus," ed. R. L. Demolen, in *Erasmus of Rotterdam: A Quincentennial Symposium* (New York: Twayne Publishers, 1971), pp. 117-119, where there is some allusion to earthly bread, but this is set aside as being unworthy to compare with the true spiritual daily bread.

[45] Erasmus, *Opera Omnia, Novum Testamentum*, vol. 6, col. 35: Erasmus discusses several patristic interpretations, but concludes: "Nec enim in precatione tam coelesti Christus de hoc, opinor, loquitur pane, quem a suis parentibus accipiunt & gentes." As Froehlich indicates, this spiritual meaning is the dominant patristic interpretation.

chisms in 1529, he had changed his view of "daily bread"[46] and adopted that of Chrysostom which Bucer had already espoused in his synoptic commentary two years previously, and which Calvin later followed.

For Bucer and Calvin, the bread for which we pray is the sustenance needed for our earthly lives. Bucer calls upon Chrysostom as support for his view that here we are to pray for food and other necessities of the body.[47] Calvin does not mention Chrysostom at this point, but his explanation of daily bread is the same as Bucer's, that is, all the things we need for this earthly life, to "eat our bread in peace." Calvin goes on to explain the value of praying for bread, in a way which might sound quite contemporary. Even if we seem able to trust God with our souls, we become anxious about our bodies,[48] so God instructs us to pray for ordinary food. Calvin maintains that once we have trusted God for this life and its necessities, we are more ready to trust God also for the gift of salvation. In 1539, Calvin objects to the interpretation of daily bread as "supersubstantial" or beyond ordinary food, because this does not seem in accord with the meaning of Jesus' words.[49] The comment is explicit but anonymous and without heat.

Calvin returns to the development of this argument in the 1550's, attacking Erasmus' remark in the *Annotations* as unbiblical. Essentially, Erasmus believes that it is inappropriate for us to think of ordinary food when we approach God, but Calvin says that this reasoning is trivial and contrary to devotion. Scripture shows us the opposite in many places: earthly good is used to lead us to hope for heavenly good. The ultimate test of faith is to trust God for everything, including the least things, the needs of our flesh.[50] Having demonstrated the biblical character of reading Christ's words about

[46] Luther, "Auslegung deutsch des Vaterunsers für einfältigen Laien," WA 2, pp. 105-116; "Betbüchlein," WA 10:2, pp. 401-403. See "Deutsch Catechismus" and "Der Kleine Katechismus," WA 30:1, pp. 203-206, 303-305; esp. p. 203 n. 1, where the editors note that in the catechism Luther has given up the meaning "panis spiritualis" which was still heard in the sermon on this petition, given on 26 May 1528. Calvin's interpretation was thus the same as that of the Luther of the catechisms. However, Bucer's usage (1527) was prior to Luther's (1529), and Luther's discussion is not developed in quite the same way as that of Bucer and Calvin. In view of this and other similarities between Bucer and Calvin (see nn. 68-69), it is probable that Calvin was influenced primarily by Bucer here also. Ganoczy, *Le jeune Calvin*, p. 175, considers the relationship among the reformers less striking in the second half of the Prayer. He seems to have missed the development of Luther's position, and the consequent remarkableness of the similarities between Bucer and Calvin, on the matter of daily bread. It is interesting to note that Valdés changes his interpretation much as does Luther; in the early *Dialogue*, p. 136, the bread is primarily doctrine, in *San Matteo*, p. 198, it is earthly sustenance.

[47] Bucer, *Enarrationes*, f65r-v, Eng. pp. 354-355. See Chrysostom, MPG 47:280.

[48] *Institutes 1536*, OS 1:111, Eng. pp. 80-81.

[49] *Institution 1541*, p. 183.

[50] *Harmony*, OC 45:199, Eng. p. 209. See Bucer, *Enarrationes*, f65r-v, Eng. pp. 354-355.

daily bread in a material sense, Calvin continues by pointing out the appropriateness of including earthly food in the perfect model prayer. If Christ had not spoken of bodily food here the prayer would be incomplete, not perfect.[51]

Perhaps because the controversy led him to defend his understanding of ordinary bread, in the commentary Calvin feels obliged to explain the relationship between this petition and those which follow. Mentioning bread before forgiveness and deliverance from evil does not mean that daily bread is more important; Christ puts the lesser petition before the greater to lead believers up from earthly matters to heavenly ones.[52]

A second part of the petition for daily bread concentrates on the meaning of "daily" and how we can call this bread "ours." Daily bread is that which is sufficient for the day, for moderate needs, not extravagance. No matter what we think we possess, we are able to enjoy it only by God's grace; all we can have will nourish us only if God so ordains, and not by any intrinsic value of the elements. Thus it is necessary that we continue to ask for daily food, even when we apparently have ample supplies.[53] This bread is also called "ours" only by God's grace, even if it comes to us by our own work and diligence. (Trusting God does not negate activity!) Our bread is that which we have earned without detriment to others; calling it ours is a warning not to desire the possessions of others.[54] The commentary intriguingly links this prayer for daily bread with the teaching on the right worship of God as well as vocation.[55] Those who ask God for their daily bread honor God as God; those who trust themselves or someone else or the abundance of their possessions both refuse to glorify God, and also deny themselves sustenance.

[51] "For we are told in many places to cast all our cares on the lap of God, and He Himself generously undertakes that He will fail us at no point. So, in a correct order of prayer ... there must be some instruction on the innumerable necessities of this present life" (*Harmony*, OC 45:199, Eng. pp. 209-210).

[52] *Harmony*, OC 45:199, Eng. p. 209. *Institutes 1559*, 3.20.44, OS 4:357, Eng. 2:908-909.

[53] *Institutes 1536*, OS 1:111, Eng. p. 81. There is some slight development in 1539, with reference to Deut. 8:3/Mt. 4:4, but substantially the idea is the same. See *Institution 1541*, p. 184. See the minority patristic position (Froehlich).

[54] *Institutes 1536*, OS 1:111, Eng. p. 81; "without detriment to others" is added in 1539 (see *Institution 1541*, p. 185).

[55] "Of course the fields are to be tilled, we must sweat over the gathering-in of the fruits of the earth, each must undergo and endure the labour of his own calling, to get himself a living, but this does not prevent us being fed by the gratuitous goodwill of God, without which men vainly wear themselves out upon their tasks. So we are taught to acknowledge at His hand all that appears to be the proceeds of our own effort. At the same time, we may understand from this utterance, that if we wish to be fed at God's hand, we must not go to another's" (*Harmony*, OC 45:200, Eng. p. 211).

"FORGIVE US OUR DEBTS, AS WE FORGIVE OUR DEBTORS." Calvin's discussion of the fifth petition includes the strongest Protestant notes. From the beginning, in 1536, until the end, the central issues are the sinfulness of all people, which makes forgiveness a constant necessity for everyone, and especially the corollary, that forgiveness is given only by the free mercy of God, without any human merits. Since Christ in this prayer commands us to pray for forgiveness throughout our life, it is obvious that those who think they do not need to repent are defying God.[56] Calvin says that there is a glimmer of righteousness in the saints, but throughout this life they are burdened with sins which require forgiveness.[57] Forgiveness comes only by God's sheer grace. There is no place for bargaining with God, as if we could deserve grace or offer something in return. Only God's gratuitous goodness can give us freedom from our debts, accepting us for Christ's sake *as if* we were innocent and just.[58]

The second part of the petition, "as we forgive our debtors," might sound like a contradiction of this insistence on our inability to earn forgiveness. Forgiving others is not a kind of condition by which we oblige God to forgive us. We cannot in fact forgive sin; only God can do that. What we must do is cast wrath and desire for revenge out of our hearts, and even seek to win the good will of our enemies.[59] Such forgiveness on our part can only be accomplished by the power of the Holy Spirit, and the presence of the Spirit in our hearts is the witness of our adoption. Our forgiving others does not earn God's forgiveness, but it is a sign or seal of our being forgiven by God, to comfort us in our weakness.[60]

"LEAD US NOT INTO TEMPTATION." For Bucer and Calvin, the prayer that we "not be led into temptation but delivered from evil" is a

[56] *Institutes 1536*, OS 1:112, Eng. pp. 81-82. Development in *Harmony*, OC 45:201, Eng. p. 211. The polemic here is directed against sectarian groups: those who believed that the church could and should be made up only of the elect, or people who took the idea of justification by faith as an excuse for immoral behavior, on the grounds that the person who has faith no longer can sin. See *Institutes 1559*, 3.20.45, OS 4:360 n. 1 (which refers to "spirituales et anabaptistae"), Eng. 2:911 n. 85 (which refers to "Libertines").

[57] *Harmony*, OC 45:201, Eng. p. 211. *Institutes 1559*, 3.20.45, OS 4:360, Eng. 2:911 indicates that God gradually restores the image of God in us, but it is never complete in this life.

[58] *Institutes 1536*, OS 1:112, Eng. pp. 81-82; developed in *Harmony*, OC 45:201, Eng. p. 212.

[59] *Institutes 1536*, OS 1:112-113, Eng. p. 82. Note here a part of Calvin's interpretation of the third use of the law, i.e., the idea that a negative implies its opposite. See *Institutes 1559*, 2.7.12-13, 2.8.6,8. Here Erasmus provides an interesting example of wavering: *Paraphrases*, vol. 7, col. 38, implies a condition; *Novum Testamentum*, vol. 6, col. 35, denies that this is a condition. There is a strong patristic tradition supporting the idea that Christ here teaches reciprocity (see Froehlich) which helps account for Calvin's insistent denial.

[60] *Institutes 1536*, OS 1:112-113, Eng. p. 82; for the reference to the Holy Spirit, see *Harmony*, OC 45:201, Eng. p. 212.

single petition with two parts. The first part deals with temptation and what it means to be led into it, and by whom.

Temptations are not evil in themselves, but they can be used by the devil for our downfall.[61] We do not pray that we may feel no temptation, because we need to be tested in order not to become lazy and sluggish. God tempts us in order to exercise our faith, and always provides a way out. The devil, who attacks the defenseless, tempts in order to destroy. We are to pray, then, not to escape all testing but to be kept from yielding and falling into sin.[62]

The theme of God's tempting is a thorny one. Bucer's struggle with the sixth petition fills almost half of the passage on the Lord's Prayer.[63] Calvin, on the other hand, treats the matter with amazing brevity, considering the opportunity it might have afforded for an investigation of predestination and reprobation. The educational aspect of God's testing of believers is the focus in 1536. A little more is said in the 1542 Catechism, where Calvin simply states that God preserves the faithful but abandons those God wishes to punish.[64] The commentary and the 1559 edition of the *Institutes* expand the discussion slightly. As regards the abandoning of some, Calvin attributes this to the secret or obscure judgment of God; he affirms that God is not the author of evil, and that God's action is just, though hidden from our understanding. Then Calvin leaves the matter there.[65]

Calvin sums up the whole sixth petition by saying that it "corresponds to the promise that the law is to be engraved upon our hearts," softening our

[61] *Institutes 1536*, OS 1:113, Eng. pp. 82-83. Some temptations are "from the right," i.e., great wealth and the good things of this life, which can distract us and tempt us to forget God. Others are "from the left," i.e., afflictions and poverty of all sorts, which can make us despair and lead to bitterness and alienation from God. Note that Calvin does not consider the good things of this life as bad in themselves. For patristic evidence for the usefulness of temptations, based on extensive cross references to other biblical examples, see Froehlich's article in this volume.

[62] *Institutes 1536*, OS 1:113-114, Eng. p. 83.

[63] Bucer, *Enarrationes*, f65v-67v, Eng. pp. 356-362. The marginalia (not in English) are expressive: tentatio duplex; Deus & qui verbum Dei docent, indurant malos; Deus inducit in tentationem; Iudicia Domini in futuro saeculo recte cognoscentur; Nostra autem peccata; Quomodo intelligendum nolo mortem impii; Vult cunctos saluari; Tentatio non deprecanda; Tentatio deprecanda; Tentatio credentibus non timenda.

[64] *Institutes 1536*, OS 1:113-114, Eng. p. 83. Catechism 1542, OC 6:105 (43rd Sunday).

[65] *Harmony*, OC 45:202, Eng. p. 213: "Certainly everyone is tempted by his own lusts, as James tells us (1.14), but as God both allows Satan's whim to inflame the fire of lust, and also uses him as the agent of His wrath when He determines to drive men headlong into destruction, thus in His own way He actually leads men into temptation. In this sense, an evil spirit of God is said to have seized upon Saul, and there are similar arguments in several passages of Scripture, not that we are on this account to start to call God the Author of evil, for His sending men along the way of the wicked is not reckless tyranny, but the execution of His righteous—though obscure—judgments." See *Institutes 1559*, 3.20.46, OS 4:363-364, Eng. 2:915.

hearts and giving us aid against "the violent assaults of Satan."[66] The reformer's viewpoint on the last two petitions of the Lord's Prayer is particularly noteworthy; in essence, the forgiveness of sins and the deliverance from yielding to evil temptation, serve as a summary of the gospel.

Now Christ has put in two petitions the objects of our soul's eternal salvation and spiritual life, as though these were the two headings of the divine covenant which comprise our whole salvation: He offers us free reconcilation, by not imputing our sins to us, and He promises the Spirit, to engrave upon our hearts the righteousness of the Law.[67]

"FOR THINE IS THE KINGDOM." The conclusion of the Lord's Prayer is treated by Calvin and others[68] as a repose for faith. The phrase is not found in the Latin, but Calvin says that it is so appropriate that it should not be omitted.[69] This doxology is a reminder that we always have a reason to pray, no matter how miserable and sinful we may be, because we know that God's kingdom, power, and glory are invincible, and thus we are safe in God's care as we could never be in our own. The "Amen" signifies a strengthened hope, that all that we ask has already come to pass, since these things have been promised by God, who cannot deceive.[70]

III. Conclusion

How might we sum up Calvin's teaching on the Lord's Prayer? First, this prayer is clearly central to his understanding of prayer in general, which

---

[66] *Institutes 1559*, 3.20.46, OS 4:361, Eng. 2:913.

[67] *Harmony*, OC 45:200, Eng. p. 211. See *Institutes 1559*, 3.20.45, OS 4:359, Eng. 2:910. Forgiveness and deliverance from evil correspond to repentance and newness of life. For these two as the summary of the gospel, the first sketch is found in 1539 (see *Institution 1541*, vol. 2, chap. 5, p. 171), but the clearest form is in the 1559 edition of the *Institutes* (see *Institutes 1559*, 3.3.1, OS 4:55, Eng. 1:592).

[68] Luther comments on the "Amen," but not the rest of the doxology, in several of his works. See "Auslegung deutsch des Vaterunsers für einfältigen Laien" (WA 2, pp. 126ff); "Betbüchlein" (WA 10:2, p. 407); "Der Kleine Katechismus" (*Enchiridion piarum precationum*) (WA 30:1, p. 308). The fact that Luther omits all except the "Amen," and Bucer includes the rest of the doxology, is one reason Ganoczy gives for attributing to Bucer the major influence on Calvin's teaching on the Lord's Prayer. See Ganoczy, *Le jeune Calvin*, p. 175, and Bucer, *Enarrationes*, f67v, Eng. p. 362. On the other hand, a note in the McNeill-Battles English edition of the *Institutes 1559*, 2:916 n. 89, suggests similarities between Calvin and Luther's phraseology on the "Amen" in his *Enchiridion*.

[69] Reference to the fact that this is not found in the Latin is added in 1539, see *Institution 1541*, p. 191. See Bucer, *Enarrationes*, f67v, Eng. p. 362, for a similar judgment about appropriateness. Erasmus, *Opera Omnia, Novum Testamentum*, vol. 7, col. 36, gives an extended argument on the subject of the source of this doxology. Bucer and Calvin are by contrast very brief and undogmatic.

[70] *Institutes 1536*, OS 1:115, Eng. p. 84.

itself is the chief exercise of our devotion, the most important practice of our worship life. The Lord's Prayer serves as a model for all right prayer, not in its precise words but in the major concerns for which we are to pray. It provides for our weakness, including all that is necessary and good to ask.

The Lord's Prayer was given to us by God's will. Because Christ is our savior, because by the power of the Holy Spirit we are adopted as children of God, we are privileged to address Christ's Father as our Father. Thus we are assured that God loves and cares for us, that the goodness and the power of God will never fail those who are Christ's sisters and brothers. We receive this promise as a body, as those who are bound together in love, and we pray in common for the whole of God's people.

The petitions of the Lord's Prayer, like all right worship, are primarily concerned with the glory and honor of God. We pray that God's name may be revered as it should be, we pray that God may be honored as God. We pray that all creation may willingly accept God's rule, that all may be brought to will as God wills. Christ also teaches us that we may and should ask our Father for the things which we need, not only spiritual and eternal, but also physical and earthly, needs. God knows that we are weak of faith if we lack daily bread, and cares for our bodies so that we may know that nothing is too small for God's love. We also pray for the two most important things we could possibly ask. The first is forgiveness for our sins, which separate us from God; the second is the presence of the Holy Spirit to create us anew in God's image and bring us safely through all evil to the final joyous fulfilment of God's kingdom, power, and glory.

Pastoral Theology and the Lord's Prayer: We Dare to Pray

by Patricia Wilson-Kastner

WHEN I was asked to deliver a paper at this conference, my initial and instinctive reaction was negative. The place of the Lord's Prayer in pastoral theology is a theme broader and deeper than the sea, and perhaps higher even than the sky. What fool would be brave enough to tackle the vast personal and corporate spiritual dimensions of the Lord's Prayer, implications of the Lord's Prayer for parish life and development, the Lord's Prayer and Christian Education, ethical ramifications of the Lord's Prayer, etc.?[1] All of these and more are encompassed in that growing family of theological concerns we call pastoral. My present effort is far less ambitious.

Three years ago, after fifteen years of seminary teaching, I accepted a call to become rector of the Church of the Resurrection, a small parish in eastern Connecticut, an economically depressed area, totally dependent on the defense industry. In these three years, we have run the gamut of pastoral encounters, encompassing such diverse activities as opening a Head Start Center in the parish hall, healing major parish conflict, and developing more personally involving styles of worship.

My intention on returning to the parish, was to become more aware of the present state of the church, and so it has happened. In composing this paper, I found myself wandering the boundary lands between apologetics and proclamation. The issues which I have addressed have emerged from my life at the Church of the Resurrection. What I offer is merely a sample of the kind of theological reflection I think many of us must continue to do. In that respect, it is more of a journal *en marche*, than a finished scholarly product. Nevertheless, it suggests a starting point.

I. PREACHING AND THE LORD'S PRAYER

Every book about preaching operates with a normative definition/description of preaching. Assuredly there is no single, totally adequate definition or description of preaching, but here are a few: "Preaching is both description and address. ... Preaching is both private and public. ...

---

[1] A basic bibliography of studies is Jean Carmignac, *Recherches sur le "Notre Père"* (Paris: Letouzey & Ané, 1969).

Preaching is both words and the Word."² "Preaching is the 'word of God' in that it participates in God's purpose, is initiated by Christ, and is supported by the Spirit with community in the world."³ "A sermonic idea is a homiletical bind; a sermon is a narrative plot!"⁴ "Preaching is an address to the worshiping community as a part of the liturgy, and thus is a part of the church's prayer to God."⁵

The list of definitions, reflections, and disagreements could go on indefinitely,⁶ proving that there is today no single universally accepted definition of preaching. There are, however, a few generally accepted principles about preaching which I want to lift up for our consideration. First, preaching is not simply an intellectual exercise. It involves the whole of the human person, intellect and affect, thinking, feeling, sensing, acting, wishing, dreaming. Second, preaching is an integral part of the worship life of the church. It is not a separate activity, sometimes inserted into a service of prayers and hymns in which it is the central attraction. Preaching is always linked to our formal or informal liturgy, directly or indirectly. Preaching is a primary bearer of our encounter with God in corporate worship. Third, because preaching is expressive of the whole person, and so intimately related to the church's worship, preaching is at the same time both a major corporate activity of the church and its members, and also highly personal and individual in the way it is heard by members of the congregation.

My point here is only that preaching is a very complex activity, both in its doing and its receiving. The preacher must, in the same act of preaching, be intellectually cogent, appeal to the emotional life of the congregation, weave together time and space, plot and sensory symbol, individual awareness, and the life and concerns of the specific community in the context of church and world. (Other than that, nothing to it!) The preacher is engaged in a constant pastoral, ethical, and theological balancing act as she or he encounters the congregation.

I underline this reality to clarify the context for my comments about the Lord's Prayer and its role in preaching. In light of what I have said, it is patently obvious that much more is at stake than how to explain effectively the different petitions, or to wonder if the pattern of the Lord's Prayer is a good one for sermons or even for the congregation's own prayer.

---

² Fred B. Craddock, *Preaching* (Nashville: Abingdon, 1985), pp. 17-18.
³ David Buttrick, *Homiletic* (Philadelphia: Fortress, 1987), p. 456.
⁴ Eugene L. Lowry, *The Homiletical Plot* (Atlanta: John Knox Press, 1980), p. 16.
⁵ Patricia Wilson-Kastner, *Imagery for Preaching* (Minneapolis: Fortress, 1989), p. 14.
⁶ Richard Lischer, *Theories of Preaching* (Durham: Labyrinth Press, 1987) offers a broad historical perspective about theories of preaching over the centuries.

The interconnection between preaching and the Lord's Prayer also needs to be explored with respect to the nature and well-being of the church. I am speaking about the Lord's Prayer because I was invited to address that topic, but as a pastor I am acutely aware of how deeply the Lord's Prayer permeates our conscious and unconscious selves. For us Episcopalians, the Lord's Prayer is part of every major Sunday worship service, whether Eucharist (always at Eucharist!) or Morning Prayer. Most Christians share that tradition, by custom or rubric.

The Lord's Prayer lies deep in the psyche of individuals and of our community. It is among the first prayers Christian children memorize. Adults delight in arguing over traditional or new translation, or at least over "sins," "debts," or "trespasses." When I visit a nursing home, or the bedside of someone who is dying, there are two prayers which are familiar to the end—Psalm 23 and the Lord's Prayer. The Lord's Prayer is often the final community prayer of someone's life, whispered, or followed silently while holding someone's hand. Our most elemental feelings as well as sophisticated theological thoughts are all bound up together in the apparently simple words of the Lord's Prayer.

Its enduring place both in liturgy and personal prayer ensures the Lord's Prayer a special status, and gives it a central place in our pastoral theological explorations. The Lord's Prayer raises many kinds of questions for us as preachers. It challenges our perspective, points us in new (or renewed directions), shapes our preaching and our listening to preaching. It also presses us to wrestle with fundamental issues about prayer, human language, and communication with and about God. I wish to explore those questions for the rest of this paper.

II. THEOLOGICAL AND PASTORAL ISSUES RAISED BY THE LORD'S PRAYER

The following points are not comprehensive, although they are assuredly interrelated. I tried instead to ask myself what I thought were the chief issues which the Lord's Prayer raises for our religious life. I did so because sermons provide the time and place in worship in which our contemporary story explicitly coincides with God's story with humanity in the scriptures. In the sermon we remember, reflect, and articulate the way in which God addresses us in order to illumine our human condition, to expose its reality, to heal, strengthen, and transform it. Thus it seems essential to look at key questions which the Lord's Prayer addresses to contemporary human reality.

Anthropomorphism. In most contemporary revisions of the Eucharistic liturgy, the traditional introduction to the prayer, "as our Savior Christ has taught us, we dare to say," has been changed to "we now pray." I confess some regret over that particular change, because it seems appropriate to me to preserve in some form the astonishment that we feel when we pray to God using human language, especially the currency of human relationship. To pray and to be heard by the God of Isaiah 6, before whom the cherubim veil their faces and the powers of heaven cry, "holy, holy, holy," is already an astonishing privilege. How much more astonishing to speak of this God in human language, using human reference points, implying that God really is in some sense like us and we like God. The Lord's Prayer, by its very anthropomorphic language, asserts its claim that humanity is in God's image, as Genesis 1:27 boldly states. It furthermore insists, through its usage of such terms, that anthropomorphic language is the proper language of prayer.

Such an approach to God is genuinely "awesome"; but it also presents the preacher with profound complications. Comparisons between God and humanity are useful to help us understand God if the human term of comparison communicates some of the good one intends to affirm about God. One can draw up criteria for the appropriateness of such language.[7] But what happens when the person or persons to whom we are preaching receive from our words exactly the opposite message from the one we wish to convey? What can we do when our language may or can convey to certain members of our congregations the image of God's anger and undependability, instead of tenderness and trust? How can we preach about "our Father" in a time when families are under great stress, and the incidence of domestic violence is rising?[8]

Even though we feel acutely the problems of human "father" language about God, we are not the first generation. For human beings, "father" is not a transparent, self-explanatory term. In 1942, Ernest F. Tittle wrote:

Simply to say that God is our Father is not enough. Among us there are all sorts of fathers, some whom could hardly serve as an illustration, much less as a symbol, of the love of God. Studdert-Kennedy once said: "When I try to tell a small boy in the slums that God is his Father, I

---

[7] I have tried to do so from a preacher's perspective in *Imagery for Preaching*, pp. 47-61.

[8] Some thought-provoking suggestions are raised by Diane Tennis, *Is God the Only Reliable Father?* (Philadelphia: Westminster Press, 1985).

often wonder what he makes of it when his idea about fathers may be that they beat mothers and are generally drunk."[9]

The point is still well taken, that to far larger numbers of people than we may imagine, and often to the preacher her- or himself, the image "father" connotes inadequacy, abusiveness, anger, and emotional and physical violence.

At the same time that the preacher encounters those for whom the anthropomorphism seems a stumbling block for an encounter with God, there are people for whom "father" bespeaks intimacy, strength, protection, and constant guiding love. Although to some people the image of "father" evokes strong negative responses, to others it offers a direct line to sensing the character of God's love towards us, of just the sort Jesus was suggesting.

What to do? Give two sermons, one for the people who had good fathers and another for those who had bad fathers? Stop using parental or any other human imagery for God? Refer to God only with abstract language which is not subject to the affective problems of anthropomorphic figures?

Most preachers do not have an honest option of this sort. If we are Christians, our tradition gives us Jesus Christ, who clearly perceives and articulates his and our relationship to God under the figure of God as our Father. That is not the only figure he uses, but there it is, right in front of us. Even if our congregations did not care, and we can be sure that most will, passionately, we must preach something about God as Father.

Perhaps it is important to begin with the question of anthropomorphism. (In the literature of prayer and spirituality this issue is discussed in relation to kataphatic and apophatic spirituality.) It is classic doctrine, embedded in the scriptures and the Christian tradition, that God is and is not what our human language calls God. Although different parts of the Bible and various theologians differ about how much difference and similarity there is, it is common currency that we can and must call God by human terms and language, and that those words correspond to a reality in God, as God is made known to us. Nevertheless, these words are merely pointers, indicators of a God whose reality is too great to be comprehended by any human person.

We need familiar human language to communicate with and to understand God. Who among us can for very long pray to God as Supreme Being, Unmoved Mover, the Ground of Being, God as primordial and consequent

[9] Ernest Freemont Tittle, *The Lord's Prayer* (New York, Nashville: Abingdon-Cokesbury, 1942), p. 13.

nature with the world, etc.? All theologies have properly abstract words and terms for God. But that vocabulary does not belong to liturgy and preaching, per se. We communicate with heart and head, and use words with intellectual content and affective dimension. So by tradition, and by the very nature of our task as preachers, we must deal with the anthropomorphism of "Father."

I have four suggestions of a practical nature. The first is that we not just call God Father in sermons, but tell stories about human fathers, and Jesus' relationship with the one he calls his Father. "Father" needs to be explained, for our theology, for our devotional life, and for our life as a human community. God as Father is a part of our religious heritage, and the preacher needs to struggle to make it accessible.

The second suggestion is that we be absolutely clear with our congregations and with ourselves that language about God is symbolic, but real, true, and important. Put differently, "God is as high above our ways as the earth above the heavens," and at the same time, God dwells among us, speaks our language, expresses the divine reality in human terms through human beings. Anthropomorphism is not, in and of itself, bad or even misleading, as long as we know what we are doing when we use it, and when we tell our congregations, directly and indirectly, that we are using human language to express the inexpressible.

My third suggestion is that we carefully balance the images we use. Scripture and tradition assure us that Jesus called God "Father." To grasp and be grasped by his sense of God's relationship to him and to us, we must experience this relationship, and to be true to Jesus' words to us, we must use the "father" image. But there are many other images of God that are equally true of God, and must also be used for a true image of God to emerge for us. We also need many images and ideas of "Abba" presented as a loving parent, in order to express what Jesus meant. To feel and to perceive his notion of "father," rather than our twentieth century projections, we will have to suggest what are in our culture motherly as well as fatherly actions, and picture a parent with love and respect for adults as well as young children.

A fourth suggestion is that the preacher show how Jesus' notion of "father" is a corrective to earthly fathers and families (Eph. 3:14-19). For us, the theological vision shapes the earthly reality we seek to create. As simple as it is to assume that we take our notion of "father" from our earthly father and revise it a bit to make it more holy, we can help people enormously by identifying how God's relationship to humanity as its "father" provides a model for human fathers and gives us a vision of what human relationships can become by God's grace.

"Our Father" and Patriarchy. Because the issue of sexism and patriarchy is so central to theological discourse globally, it needs separate treatment from the general question of anthropomorphism. Today in our contemporary Western theology (and in some Asian and African theologies) one burning issue overshadows all others. Can we who are struggling against the destructive and sinful effects of patriarchy call God "our Father"? How dare we encourage others to call God Father and thus perpetrate the negative effects of patriarchy? This emotionally laden issue has produced every shade of opinion, from radical feminist theorists like Mary Daly and Daphne Hampson who assert that Christianity is intrinsically and irredeemably patriarchal and sexist, to conservatives like William Oddie, who respond with horror, identifying all feminists with the most extreme opinions, and assume that all people who question exclusively male language about God are out to destroy the Christian tradition and belief in God.[10]

I am not here to recapitulate the debate, or to offer my own perspectives.[11] In a Christian worshiping community, the preacher must face the reality that in the majority of congregations, most shades of opinion are present, with most people probably having strong feelings but not much education about the issue, especially about biblical usage. The debate, and much of the background work, belongs in classes, I firmly believe, not in the pulpit. However, even if one observes those distinctions, the preacher still has to decide how to preach about God the Father to a given congregation.

[10] It would take a book to list and evaluate the contemporary literature about God the Father, gender, and liturgical language. I will not attempt to do so, but will suggest as a fair sample of the vast literature available: Leonardo Boff, *The Maternal Face of God* (San Francisco: Harper and Row, 1987); Jann Aldredge Clanton *In Whose Image?* (New York: Crossroad, 1990); Mary Daly, *Beyond God the Father* (Boston: Beacon Press, 1973); Ruth Duck, *Gender and the Name of God* (New York: Pilgrim Press, 1991); Robert G. Hamerton-Kelly, *God the Father: Theology and Patriarchy in the Teaching of Jesus* (Philadelphia: Fortress, 1979); Daphne Hampson, *Feminism and Theology* (London: Basil Blackwell, 1990); Margaret Hebblethwaite, *Motherhood and God* (London: Godfrey Chapman, 1984); Marianne Katoppo, *Compassionate and Free* (Maryknoll: Orbis, 1979); William Oddie, *What Will Happen to God?* (London: SPCK, 1984); Gail Ramshaw, *Worship: Searching for Language* (Washington: Pastoral Press, 1988); W. A. Vissert 't Hooft, *The Fatherhood of God in an Age of Emancipation* (Philadelphia: Westminster Press, 1982). The preacher who steps up into the pulpit to preach about "our Father" needs to be familiar with at least some of the depth and the breadth of the literature and of the theological issues under dispute. Otherwise one runs the danger of misrepresenting a complex issue, unnecessarily alienating instead of illumining and helping people, and looking very foolish. I have heard preachers achieve all of these goals.

[11] My major effort to do so was in my *Faith, Feminism, and the Christ* (Philadelphia: Fortress, 1983).

The preacher needs to juggle several realities. One is that Jesus calls God "Abba." Jesus is a male in a patriarchal society. That is a given which provides him with his emotional and conceptual framework, and it sets certain parameters to his thought and expressions. Jesus expresses himself in familiar language and concepts in ways which challenge the fundamental assumptions of patriarchy. At the same time, his is still the challenging, inclusive, and radical language of a male in a patriarchal society. We cannot turn Jesus into a twentieth century feminist in first century Jewish robes.

Another reality for the preacher is that everyone in the congregation who was raised a Christian grew up saying the Lord's Prayer. Everyone has strong emotional ties to it. As we have already recognized, various people experience a wide range of reactions to "our Father." Some people love it because it reminds them of their fathers, some because it speaks of a close and compassionate relationship to God, some because they have struggled to an intimate paternal relationship with God after bad relationships with their human fathers. Others hate the Prayer because it reminds them of their fathers, some because it seems to affirm men, whom they mistrust and hate, some because it sounds symbolic of oppressive patriarchy. Everyone feels deeply. "Father" resonates with the roots of our sense of self, and our relationships in family, society, and religious structures. The preacher can escape neither the profundity of the feelings nor the responsibility of preaching about God as "Abba, Father."

What to say and do? The preacher must be honest and aware of her or his own feelings and beliefs. My own approach is to preach about "our Father, Abba" as Jesus' own experience of God. It expresses a vision of intimacy and trust, I say, not a primary focus on maleness. Jesus was a man in a world in which the father was the head and provider. I try to explain Jesus' experience, as best I can, his context, and his relationship to God extended to us. I use Jesus' language, and also contemporary language, and say that we need to imagine also mother-child relationships to gain the full sense of God's parental love for us. I try to connect Jesus' language and articulated experience with what we today might say and feel.

I think it is much more important and true to Jesus' own person and mission to communicate his sense of "Abba" as God's life-giving and creative love present and freely given to us, than to spend a great deal of time insisting on Father as a primary image for God. At the same time, I am very straight-forward with people that Father is Jesus' major image and name for God, he invites us to share this relationship, and uses these words. My preaching, I trust and pray, reflects a desire to be faithful to scripture and tradition; a conviction that the God-language of the scriptures is symbolic, not literal or designating the nature of God; and an intention to communicate the gospel as best I can with the specific congregation to which I am preaching.

Transcendence and Immanence. In Matthew's, Luke's, or the ecclesiastical version of the Lord's Prayer, we find a very clear distinction: the Father is in heaven, and the reign of the Father is to be on earth as in heaven. The rest of the prayer reflects this same distinction. Anyone who reads contemporary theology knows that any distinction between God and the world is being challenged today as vigorously as ever before in Christian history. From the perspectives of feminist, liberation, process, and other theologies, many cries arise to dispense with what are deemed false separations of reality into a two or three tiered universe. God and the world, if one even makes those distinctions, are one reality.

The distinctions are challenged just as bluntly in everyday life for non-philosophically inclined people. The dominant culture mocks any vital belief in anything beyond "what you see is what you get." If God and heaven are admitted at all into popular discourse, they are for life after death, certainly not for "on earth as in heaven." Interpreting and reinterpreting, demythologizing, the Lord's Prayer seems to fall by the way, as outmoded, or at best wedded to an archaic or classical world view. No matter how one interprets it, however, the issue of transcendence and immanence, in some form or other, seems so intrinsic to the Lord's Prayer as to be inseparable from it.

The framework of immanence/transcendence, however, is helpful in understanding the divine/human interrelationship from the perspective of distance, as Brazilian theologian Leonardo Boff notes. But more is needed to express the full vision of the Lord's Prayer. He suggests transparency to describe the presence and interconnection of divine and human to each other.[12] Certainly the phrasing of the coming of God's *basileia* on earth as it is in heaven bespeaks a universe in which divine and human are indeed distinct realities, but in which they interconnect and interpenetrate each other. Jesus teaches his disciples to pray that the two realities be drawn more closely together, not separated or collapsed into each other.

To pray the Lord's Prayer is to confront directly a worldview in which earthly and heavenly, God and humanity, are integrally and intimately in-

[12] Leonardo Boff, *The Lord's Prayer: The Prayer of Integral Liberation* (Maryknoll: Orbis Books, 1983), pp. 1-2.

terconnected with each other, but are not identical. In the immediate praying of the words, the believer professes faith in a God who is infinite and
unreachable and "closer than your jugular vein." The Prayer assumes that
God is absolutely the source and governor of all, and at the same time totally
present to the one who prays. The very beginning of the Prayer challenges
the preacher about the congregation's fundamental belief, his or her own
most radical convictions, and the actuality of these beliefs in shaping weekly
preaching.

Eschatology. "Hallowed be your name. Your kingdom come, your will be
done." The Lord's Prayer proclaims God's presence in everyday life, but it
also looks forward to God's action completing and perfecting the dynamic
movement of the world towards fulfillment in God. Whatever else one may
mean by eschatology, it certainly includes the notion that the world has a
purpose, whose reality and significance lie in the world's interconnection
with God. God's purpose is not yet complete on earth; the cosmos has not
yet reached its telos. Paul utters the great human call of hope and frustration
in Romans 8, speaking of the world crying and groaning in travail, waiting
to be delivered by God.

Apart from those Christians whose theological predilections run to the
grandly apocalyptic, most Christians think very little about eschatology.
They are apt to identify it with "my hope of or lack of or rejection of life
after death." Popular literature of a semi-scientific character is divided about
survival after death, and the supportive new age material suggests an individual survival that has virtually nothing to do with biblical belief. Popular
religious questions tend to be about the self, friends, family, and perhaps
pets.

In sharp contrast, the language of the Lord's Prayer is all plural, not
singular, about the community of all creation. New Testament eschatology
is cosmic, and the Lord's Prayer shares that perspective. Here again, we
strike an opposing chord from contemporary culture. Much contemporary
scientific writing denies the purposefulness or inherent intelligibility of the
cosmos. According to these theorists, we do not affect nor are we directly
affected by the universe except through impersonal natural forces. At best
we can know about, appreciate, and even feel connected to the world as one
small part of it. But the universe has no purpose, and we do not participate
in any meaningful way in its ultimate fate. We have read about competing
theories of the Big Bang or alternating contractions to explain where we
came from and what will happen to our world. No wonder that a reactive

and usually threatened individualism and anthropocentrism rule our eschatology, if we or our congregations have one at all.

"Hallowed be your name; your will be done, on earth as in heaven" directly challenges the ways in which we relate contemporary cosmologies and perspectives on world history to our preaching of the Christian vision. Whatever else is asked of us, we must in all honesty face the question of how our preaching acknowledges or refuses to admit the cosmic sovereignty of God, the purposefulness of the world (its teleology), and our human participation in that drama. A purely individual or even simply human approach is inadequate to the scope of the Lord's Prayer, as is a perspective which asserts that the world and we as individuals have no purpose.

Such an eschatology is not a cry for God to come and deliver us from the present age and whisk us off to the age to come; it is a commitment to dedicate ourselves to bringing to birth the realm of God on earth. We pledge ourselves to hallow God's name, undertaking to hallow God through our words and deeds, and laboring to bring God's realm from heaven down to earth. The eschatology of the Lord's Prayer does not simply gaze into the future; it presses us to live the ethics of God's realm on earth, in which we are brothers and sisters of one Father. Our preaching is challenged to draw explicit connections between the vision of God and the world God intends and wills, and our behavior is directed to bring about the realization of God's world. Such eschatology is not a "realized" or a "future" eschatology, but might be best termed an eschatology "in the process of being realized."

This kingdom/reign/realm of God is a realm of justice and faithful love, peace and truth. All of the qualities of God's justice and faithfulness governing our relationships with each other and with God are encompassed by this small but powerful phrase. One of the great services a preacher can offer a congregation is a readiness to proclaim God's worldly realm as a divine gift which we are already receiving, but which has not yet been brought to maturity among us. With fearless candor, the preacher must identify injustice and absence of love, and guide us in labor for God's realm even where the earthly realm is most resistant. In God's name the preacher can assure us that God's realm will come on earth, regardless of our present conflict and distress.

Such a conviction necessitates a belief in a God actively involved in our world, who expects our involvement in return. But what can we make of an interactive God and universe in a culture whose popular scientific world vision discounts or denies such a perspective?

Belief in an Involved God. "Our Father . . . give us . . . forgive us . . . save us from . . . deliver us. . . ." The God of the Lord's Prayer is no deistic Supreme Being. God is right there, present with the members of the community, listening and acting, caring about the least deed of the least significant person, as well as about the fate of the cosmos. God the Father acts graciously, justly, and compassionately towards human beings, is present to them, cares about their concerns, and interacts with them. Such an assertion is essential to the Lord's Prayer, but it also shapes Jesus' sense and idea of prayer.

"What is prayer?" is a venerable and complicated question which cannot be answered simply. It is assuredly no accident that the earliest treatises on the Lord's Prayer, such as those of Cyprian, Tertullian, and Origen, are located in the context of a general treatment of prayer. The Lord's Prayer presses us to ask ourselves very directly what we believe about God and prayer. Is prayer a training-ground for us, to make us more virtuous, but having no direct relationship to God? Is prayer direct communication with God? Why ask God for anything if God already knows what we want and need? Does God want and expect us to pray?

A great deal of Enlightenment Christianity reduced prayer to an exercise of worship in which we articulate noble sentiments about God and virtue to each other. The pietism of American religious sentiment often is expressed in the kind of individualized piety in which prayer is our expression of our desires and needs to a God who is ready to shower on us the blessings we so richly deserve. Many other kinds of prayer live in the American psyche, and ought not to be demeaned. Prayer can be a way of survival in intolerable circumstances, whether of poverty, illness, or other oppression; God gives strength where no human resources exist. Certainly more people pray than ever darken the door of church or synagogue; we need to find out much more about their prayer—its strengths and weaknesses—and to interconnect ourselves with them when and where we can.

The Lord's Prayer insists that when we pray (not as just a solitary "I," but as a member of Jesus' community) we touch God and God's power to create and recreate. Prayer "changes the world and it changes what is possible to God."[13] Prayer changes us by opening us up to God's action, thus making it possible for God to act through us to transform the world, Walter Wink asserts. For the preacher and for the congregation, the reality of the prayerful interconnection between God and us is the root of all further development of our preaching and teaching about the Lord's or any other

[13] Walter Wink, "Prayer and the Powers," *Sojourners* (October 1990): 13.

prayer. The Lord's Prayer challenges us to grapple with this root conviction of the New Testament world-view and to explore when and how we find God involved in our lives.

A God Who Wills Intimacy with Us. I have already explored for this paper some of the implications of the enormous contemporary debate in feminist theology about God and gender as that affects preaching about "our Father." It appears fairly certain, however, that Jesus was not concerned with masculine or feminine in God, but the intimate character of his and his disciples' relationship with God.[14]

Of all the names or titles possible, Jesus addressed God as Father, Abba. Jesus certainly was not suggesting sentimental childishness in our relationship with God. The term Abba does, however, emerge from a family context, and suggests a mix of affection, respect, mutual responsibilities, and love. The radical character of Jesus' giving of "Abba" as an address to God lies in its astonishing claim about the relationship of the Holy One of Israel to the disciples. The Lord's Prayer unflinchingly insists that the same God who is creator, infinitely greater than we are, capable of delivering us or not, forgiving us or not, and of bringing the world to its consummation, can also be addressed by us with the easy intimacy of a child with its parents. Obedience and confidence, affection and discipline, certain faith and eager service describe the relationship with God as Abba.[15]

Of course, in preaching, just as in good theology, one cannot merely assume that twentieth century notions of intimacy and parent-child relations are the same as first century. But as Jeremias insists, "Jesus himself regarded this childlike form of address to God as the heart of that revelation which had been granted him from the Father."[16] God is as dependable, nurturing, and actively just for us as a father is for his child. (We remember that in the ancient Near East some of the characteristics we regard as maternal would have been attributed to the father.) Jesus says that not only is God so disposed to us, but we have the right to depend absolutely on that relationship. In the same way, God-Abba is the focus of the disciples' absolute obedience and love.

[14] See, e.g., Hamerton-Kelly, *God the Father*; Ramshaw, *Worship*; Duck, *Gender and the Name of God*; Joachim Jeremias, *The Lord's Prayer* (Philadelphia: Fortress, 1964), pp. 17-21.

[15] I am indebted to Martina S. Gnadt from Princeton, for her constructive comments about this section of the paper. For a useful summary of the notion of Abba in Jesus' teaching, see Hamerton-Kelly, *God the Father*, pp. 20-81.

[16] Jeremias, *The Lord's Prayer*, p. 20.

Contemporary psychology has spent a good bit of energy in investigating various human needs and drives, and how and where we satisfy them. One fascinating theory suggests that religion deals with our dependency—our sense of limitation and mortality, and lack of control over the most fundamental dimensions of our lives.[17] This feeling of dependency is regarded as our recognition of truth about ourselves: that we are mortal and finite, and much of what is most important to us is beyond our control. To acknowledge our dependency is not pathology, but sanity. Dependency becomes pathological when it is misplaced to an inappropriate situation or person, or when it paralyzes us.

Schleiermacher, we remember, articulated religious consciousness as our awareness of "absolute dependence, or, which is the same thing, being in relationship with God."[18] It seems important that when Schleiermacher wanted to identify the core of religious feeling, not ontology, he chose radical and absolute dependence for humans, as the foundation and beginning of all other religious feeling and action. Obviously nineteenth century theology and twentieth century psychology are not identical. But they are related in their perception of religious identity, and point us to that fundamental reality with which the Lord's Prayer is concerned—the character of our dependence on God.

In a period in which there is a strong theological drift away from transcendence, parental imagery, or any counter-voice to human self-sufficiency, the Lord's Prayer sounds a strong note of affirmation to human interdependence on divine power (*dynamis* and *exousia*) as the true state of affairs. The only question for the believer is about the character of the relationship: whether it is the abject fear of a servant, the radical terror of a helpless creature in a faceless and hostile cosmos, or the trust of a child in a loving parent. The Lord's Prayer does not say that this is the only sort of relationship possible with God, but it does insist that parent-child interconnection is the bedrock of every other way we relate to God.

The preacher thus will grapple with the true meaning of the parent-child relationship with God for people of all ages, and how it relates to the other dimensions of our relationship with God. But the preacher is also pressed to confront head on the many aspects of our dependence, our mistaken efforts to satisfy that need, and how God is able to let us be as dependent as we in

[17] A. Wesley Carr, "Irrationality in Religion," in *Irrationality in Social and Organizational Life*, ed. James Krantz (Washington: A. K. Rice Institute, 1987), pp. 76-90.

[18] Friedrich Schleiermacher, *The Christian Faith* (Edinburgh: T & T Clark, 1928, 1960), pp. 12-18.

truth are, and to respond to us with parental, supportive love. Such love empowers us and frees us to be the mature heirs and adults we are capable of becoming. Acknowledgement of our dependence allows us to be maturely interdependent, instead of letting us pretend autonomy or misplace our dependency needs on another.

Community. Today we in the United States live in an atmosphere of anxiety about the foundations and the future of our community. This theme is a dominant one in public discourse, as well as theological discussion.[19] Perhaps the chief common theme is that we have lost the community of common values and concern for the common good which were soil and root to our nation. For a variety of reasons we are disintegrating as a nation. This fear is not merely a concern about pluralism; it is a growing dread that we as a people have no values but self-preservation.

Analysis of the political system comes up with the common complaint that we have lost leadership and vision as a nation. Polls and surveys portray a people who only a handfull of years ago thought that they were making slow progress but now believe that life is going backwards. Various groups of Americans may offer quite different and even inconsistent versions of their fears, but blacks, Hispanics, native Americans, white working-class, family farmers, and the amorphous "shrinking middle-class" all express a sense of economic and social free-fall. Life seems to them to have no foundations and roots, no horizon they can see, and no hope for the future.

To this fearsome cry the Lord's Prayer offers a distinct set of values with a hope inaccessible in the present society. "Our Father" is the source and the goal of all people—we are one family with a common divine originator. Because we have one Father, we are brothers and sisters of one another. Care for one another—justice and charity—are not options for a society; they are essential because God is the God of all the world.

With such an insight the Lord's Prayer challenges us in our beliefs and in our resistance. The preacher identifies the malady of the American spirit as being our cognitive assent to the existence of some vague deity. Our resistance to God's will, however, both as a nation and as individuals is rooted in our pretense to live as though we believed. What would belief in the God of the Lord's Prayer look like as played out in our common life? What would it mean to formulate a national medical or educational policy based

[19] Some of the most powerful explorations of this theme are Alan Ehrenhalt, *The United States of Ambition* (New York: Random House, 1991); E. J. Dione, *Why Americans Hate Politics* (New York: Simon and Schuster, 1991); Robert N. Bellah, et al., *Habits of the Heart* (New York: Harper and Row, 1985).

on the reality of our being brothers and sisters of a common divine Father? The gospel offers us many different dimensions of sharing for our common good—e.g., the loaves and fishes, and Jesus' sharing of his own life with the disciples. The preacher certainly has rich possibilities for weaving some of the specifically Christian sense of responsibility for one another in our common life.

Such a revival of public discourse in which values, policies, and practice are openly discussed would also uncover in us our buried common faith: "Your kingdom come; your will be done on earth as in heaven." American civil religion is not dead; it has been hurt by the corporate shock of Vietnam, political scandal, and business corruption. But for most Americans, the preacher suggests, our cynicism is the bitter disappointment of the disillusioned idealist. One of the preacher's chief tasks is to place before us the faith that God's kingdom can come on earth, and that each and all of us have a role to play, no matter how small. How do we live with the kingdom in process? Americans have always been impatient; the preacher may well introduce some important biblical metaphors we Americans have not taken seriously for the coming of the kingdom—sowing the seed and leavening the dough.

Evil and Danger in Our Present World. One of the still lively assumptions in popular culture is our Enlightenment belief that if we just try hard enough to be good, or if we can only learn enough, evil will be eliminated. The Lord's Prayer presents a different vision of our world. The reign of God is coming, but it is not yet on earth as in heaven. Three of the four petitions are directed to the reality of evil among us: "Forgive us our sins, as we forgive those who sin against us. Save us from the time of trial, and deliver us from evil."

We are sinners in need of God's forgiveness, just as others sin against, and must be forgiven by us. We are directed to see a world in which we are interconnected in a web of evil, which only through God's grace can be transformed into a network of forgiveness. No intimation of a state of perfection for us or anyone else is suggested. We are reminded of Luther's notion of *simul justus et peccator.* Evil will remain in this life, but we can escape from its chains by forgiveness, by breaking out of our resentment, anger, envy, and nursing of grudges.

Probably most Christians know that they engage in that which they ought not to do, and fail to do that which they ought to do. The Lord's Prayer points clearly to the reality of sin which is a constant part of life, and will continue to be. We will always be facing the dangers of temptation/trial/

apostasy, and need to be delivered from evil. Perhaps preachers need to be as honest with their congregations. Evil is within us, constantly around us, luring and tempting us, and we are constantly in need of forgiveness.

As Leonardo Boff notes, "The reality encompassed in the Lord's Prayer is not a pretty picture but one of heavy conflict. Here the kingdom of God confronts the kingdom of Satan."[20] The Lord's Prayer describes a world in which neither the naive supernaturalism of the fundamentalist nor the cheery optimism of the liberal is adequate. It is a world of holocausts and genocidal massacres, of growing embittered underclasses and homelessness in the midst of wealthy cities, of blasphemies and lies. In such a universe, the Lord's Prayer both alerts us to the profound and all-pervasive reality of evil, and assures us of God's care and protection in the midst of such a world.

Human Freedom and Responsibility. Connected with the issue of evil is that of human freedom and responsibility. From the angry cries of citizens who feel that they have no voice in their governance, to the overwhelming amazement of those astronomers who describe a world in which we humans are tiny helpless specks of matter, the dominant note of our society is our individual and corporate helplessness. We talk about our victimization, all the forces which shaped us, the genetic code which predestines us, and the psychological stress which destroys our decision-making ability. At the same time we struggle with self-definition, breaking free of co-dependency, and development of the self. On a broader social scale, we are aware of various interlocked systems of oppression, and we do not know how national or global societies can be delivered or what we as individuals can do.

To such a world view, the Lord's Prayer speaks of human freedom and responsibility. Powerful forces of evil are active, within and without us. But, within the limits of creatureliness and sinfulness, we can choose to sanctify God's name or to blaspheme it, to forgive or to maintain enmity, to labor for justice and peace or to be sucked into the powers of spiritual and material oppression. The underlying assumption of the Prayer is that our relationship with God empowers and frees us. We are able to make choices and to be responsible. Indeed, if we pray the Prayer as Jesus tells us, as children of Abba, we will faithfully love and serve God and actively resist evil. As Boff writes: "Any genuine liberation, from the Christian standpoint, starts with a deep encounter with God that moves us to committed action."[21]

The Lord's Prayer confronts the preacher with a world in which we are

[20] Boff, *The Lord's Prayer*, p. 5.
[21] Ibid., p. 6.

neither helpless victims nor capable of doing whatever we will. We are free, but limited, responsible but facing terrible powers of evil ranged against our obedience to the one Jesus empowers us to call "Father." In some contexts, for instance, Latin America or South Africa, the identity of the powers seems pretty clear, and the path of resistance more obvious. In others, to which we may be closer, the issues are murkier, but in their own way, present us with just such a struggle with good and empowerment to obey God's will.

The preacher's role is to present the context of freedom, struggle, and transformation, and to clarify the situations in which we live our Christian life, with its challenges and ambiguities. How am I free to act, for example, if I am a welder, with a large family to support, in a part of the country where the only jobs available are in the defense industry? What is my freedom? What is the evil with which I wrestle? What is the hope of the realm of God coming on earth as in heaven? The preacher is counseled by the Lord's Prayer to console and strengthen with confidence in Abba, as well as to illumine our encounters with evil and destructiveness in the world, and our responsibilities.

All which I have written here is a mere beginning, which attempts to suggest some ways in which the Lord's Prayer challenges us, and gives us shape and direction for our preaching. I have barely begun to address certain crucial issues, and have not undertaken a careful consideration of others, such as the coming of the reign of God. I make my own the prayer of Tertullian, sexist as he was, to the readers of his treatise on the Lord's Prayer. "Pray for me, that I shall receive from God more and more inspired thoughts . . . so as to treat the subject again and do better justice to its grandeur and sublimity. . . . But for now do read this with your kindly indulgence."[22]

[22] Tertullian, "Prayer," in *Prayer, Exhortation to Martyrdom*, Ancient Christian Writers Series (New York: Newman Press, 1954), pp. 139-140.

The Theology and Ethics of the Lord's Prayer

by DOUGLAS JOHN HALL

THERE MUST be very little in the realm of theology, which always walks close to blasphemy, that could approach the degree of presumption contained in the title of the address that I am about to offer. The theology and ethics of the Lord's Prayer! Before such a Matterhorn one feels very small indeed! Which is after all probably a very salutary posture for anyone, especially for theologians, and more especially still for "systematic" theologians!

All the same, the prospect of achieving anything remotely profound in the face of such an assignment is certainly slim; and I must assume that we are all entirely aware of that, and ready to forgive the presumption. "The Lord's Prayer and the Ten Commandments," wrote Luther, "teach more than all the councils teach."[1] There is literally no end to the theological and ethical reflection that has been and could still be inspired by this most universal prayer and verbal symbol of the Christian church. Accordingly, I have decided to concentrate these remarks on three aspects of the subject: (1) the inseparability of theology and ethics as this is demonstrated in the Prayer; (2) the integration of the public and the personal dimensions of its theology and ethic; and (3) the Prayer's fearless realism about the human condition and its equally daring hope for the world's transformation.

There are two reasons for this choice: *first*, I wanted to approach my assignment *as a theologian*; and for me this must mean seeking to become the place where text and context intersect. One's context does not determine the *content* of one's theological response, but it *does* determine the character of the concern that one brings to the contemplation of the tradition.

Yet even on the grounds of contextuality in theology there would be no end to the questions that one might carry to such a textual tradition as the Lord's Prayer. Therefore I have induced from the topic as assigned the assumption—and this is the *second* reason for my choice of the three topics named above—that what I am being asked to consider here is in particular the *intersection or interface of theology and ethics*: that is, not the theology and

[1] "On the Councils and the Churches" (1539), in *Works of Martin Luther*, Philadelphia Edition (Philadelphia: Muhlenberg Press, 1931), vol. 5, p. 252.

the ethics of the Lord's Prayer as separate and independent dimensions but rather the matters which emerge as soon as we realize that theology and ethics are inextricably interwoven.

I. The Theological Basis of the Ethic and the Ethical Thrust of Theology

The Lord's Prayer begins, as prayer almost by definition must do, with the contemplation of the divine. Human beings in their finitude and frustration, or in moments of unaccustomed ecstacy, or simply in their mysterious need to register their presence with an elusive eternity, universally invoke the transcendent. There is perhaps no greater evidence of the truth of Augustine's most famous sentence—*Tu fecisti nos ad te, Domine, et inquietum est cor nostrum donec requiescat in te*[2]—than is provided by the universality of prayer. Prayer cuts across all the divisions of human society; it supercedes doctrine and ideology; it outlasts religion itself. Possibly prayer of the most basic, most primitive and radical sort is more prevalent in the post-religious, secular societies of our world today than was the case in the ages of belief, when it could be thought "natural" to pray.

A moving tableau from the play, *Endgame*, by Samuel Beckett, poet laureate of the age which mourns the death of God,[3] illustrates my meaning: one of the characters, Hamm, proposes "Let us pray to God." They clasp their hands and close their eyes: "Our Father which art—" They wait. There is only silence. "The bastard! He doesn't exist!" says Hamm.[4] We are programmed to pray, and we do pray even when we have ceased believing that there is anything, anyone to which or to whom our subjective need objectively corresponds. The quest for transcendence is that strong in us.

But just here we encounter what seems to me the principle distinction between the prayer that rises spontaneously from the human spirit and prayer as Jesus taught it to his first followers. Characteristically, with human prayer, whether it is articulate or inarticulate, whether it is premised on belief in deity or on the atheist's incapacity wholly to dispense with "the search for ultimate reality" (Tillich), there is an unmistakable bid for escape. The quest for transcendence is always, at least in part, a Babel-quest: "Let us build a tower reaching into the heavens . . . lest we be scattered." Life in this world, the life of creatures, is "a perilous journey" (Iris Murdoch). Who has not understood the comi-tragic plea of twentieth century pop-art, "Stop

[2] "You created us for yourself, Lord, and our hearts are restless until they rest in you" (*Confessions*, bk. 1, par. 1).
[3] According to *TIME* magazine, reporting on Beckett's being awarded the Nobel Prize for literature in 1969.
[4] New York: Grove Press, 1958, pp. 53-54.

the world, I want to get off!'"? "It is appalling, the burden that man bears, the *experiential* burden," wrote Ernest Becker in one of the truly wise studies of our time, *The Denial of Death*.[5] Not so much the terror of death as the terror of life itself impells most of us to seek some sphere of peace, security and permanence beyond the *fluxus*. It is the essence of "religion," this search, and, as so much of the piety, the hymnology, the preaching and practice of religion in our context makes evident, the Christian religion is by no means immune to the temptation to offer itself precisely as supply to that perennial demand! "Jesus" becomes our guide and way out of the world.

But the Way that Jesus *truly* is, and therefore the way of prayer that he teaches, is the very antithesis of religion thus understood. Truly, the *Pater noster* begins with the contemplation of God. It is "theocentric." The human mind and spirit are permitted to do what they are in any case bound to do, in one way or another—to turn towards the transcendent other, the one who is "in heaven." But immediately—*immediately*!—the escapist propensities of the human heart by which prayer is habitually inspired are thwarted. They will not find a refuge here! For the "Father" who is invoked is "*our* Father," is turned towards "us," and in all the specificity of our worldly condition. Even "heaven," which for so many is the final solace for earth's irredeemable sorrows, does not represent an unworldly or transworldly reality here; it is part of creation: "In the beginning God created *the heavens* and the earth."

Perhaps the greatest irony of religion, and notably of the Christian religion, lies in just this strange juxtaposition: history is full of the human search for God, and of the ecstatic testimonies of those who believed they found God. But God, as biblical faith presents deity, is meanwhile preoccupied with a profound, parental search for lost humanity. *God is not God-centered*! And the God-centered have always to contend with this frustration of their designs on God. To seek and to find *this* God is to be turned back immediately, *with* God, towards the world that is beloved of God, towards the very thing that one tried, through prayer, to flee.

So our Lord's Prayer, like the opening verse of Genesis, spends very little time on God-talk—or rather, it devotes no time at all to the subject of God *in se*; for with the tradition of Jerusalem as a whole this prayer knows nothing of a "God" who is not God-with-us. As Karl Barth, the great twentieth century champion (many would allege) of God's ineffable transcendence, wrote in his exegesis of this same prayer:

[5] New York: Macmillan Publishing Co., Free Press, 1973, p. 51.

Even if there are human beings without God, there is, from the Christian viewpoint, no God without human beings. It is most important for us to understand this. God has been with us; he is with us: Emmanuel! He permits us, he commands us to pray . . . for the success of his cause. He invites us to participate in his work. . . . God invites us to join his designs and his action. And let us note that this invitation comes at the beginning and is repeated at the end, in the doxology.[6]

Quite naturally, therefore, the prayer carries all who make it their own from God into God's world: "may thy name be hallowed"—by all creatures, by human creatures especially, who hold sacred what is not sacred and squander their "ultimate concern" (Tillich) on what is not ultimate; "may thy will be done"—in a world that bows to the wills of the wilful; "may thy kingdom come *on earth*." Not for an instant is the soul permitted the *kind* of repose in God that it (understandably enough!) seeks. Prayer, if we follow *this* prayer, means thinking our way *into* God's world, not out of it![7]

But of course it is into *God's* world that Jesus' prayer intends to lead us. And that makes all the difference. We are not met here by a hard, demanding deity, the self-made-man image of a god who thinks it best for his offspring to face the music themselves, swim or sink—fight your own battles! get tough! you'll get no favors here! (The allusion here is to secularism and, in a measure, to that theology of secularity which had a certain vogue in the 1960's.) This Father does not give his child a stone when he asks for bread. Having turned to "our Father," we are not turned back, turned out. We return to the world . . . *accompanied*. The darkness we have found there is (we know it now) inhabited. If we have, here and there, now and then, the courage to be in that still-frightening place, that garden-become-wilderness; if sometimes we may even rejoice and be glad about being there, it is because "we are not alone," as the new creed of my denomination has insightfully put it; "we live in *God's* world." If we may and must busy ourselves now with the sanctifying of God's name in the world, and the doing of God's will, and the establishment of God's reign "in earth as it is in heaven," it is not under the burden of a utopianism in relation to which our efforts must always seem paltry and frequently fail; it is as *participants* in a work that is "going on," that has been under way long before our appearance on the scene and will long outlast our best, most faithful stewardly endeavors. "*God is at work in the world, to make and to keep human life human*"—Paul

---

[6] *Prayer*, ed. D. E. Saliers, 2d ed. (Philadelphia: Westminster Press, 1985), p. 48.

[7] See my *When You Pray: Thinking Your Way into God's World* (Valley Forge: Judson Press, 1987).

Lehmann's beautiful formulation of the theological basis of Christian ethics.[8]

So we encounter once more, what we can in fact never fail to encounter if we pay attention to the scriptures and best traditions of this faith: namely, the inseparability of theology and ethics. Without the theological *foundation*—that is, that God is present and graciously active already, performing precisely what we are called to take upon ourselves—the ethic devolves into the worst kind of legalism and moralism: hallowing the name becomes a pietistic judgment of all profanation and scatology; doing the will of "the Father" becomes obedience to patriarchally conceived codes of behavior and usually, in reality, the faithful maintenance of the status quo; building the kingdom becomes a program, riddled with "issues" and schemes, unforgiving of leisure, rife with righteousness! *"With God* all things are possible!" The ethic presupposes the theology; the indicative precedes the imperative—and there is some considerable danger today, I think, that many in and around the churches have forgotten this!

But woe unto those who do not know that the converse is also true. The Lord's Prayer, which in the churches we repeat so unthinkingly, commits us to this world in the most concrete and unrelenting ways. To this world *as God's world*—and therefore *not* as we would have it but as God would have it ("*thy* will be done"), not as it is, but as it is becoming ("*thy* kingdom come"). For (and I shall develop this in the third section) as it is, earth is not as it should be. God will "mend it (Fackenheim). And God will have us participate in its mending. Every time we pray this prayer we commit ourselves anew to that eternal covenant.

II. The Public and the Personal Dimensions of the Prayer

The second observation that I should like to offer on the subject of the theology and ethics of this prayer concerns another matter about which, it seems to me, there is a good deal of confusion in the Christian movement today, and particularly in the once-mainline churches. I refer to the public and the personal dimensions of the faith, and the confusion about which I am thinking is the seeming incapacity of so much contemporary Christianity to sustain these dimensions simultaneously—*dialectically*, of course—but within the framework of their *inherent* tensions, and not because of the extraneous priorities, distinctions and polarities that we visit upon them on account of our conflicting orientations, preferences, and ideologies.

There are, happily, exceptions to this generalization, but a conspicuous

[8] *Ethics in a Christian Context* (New York and Evanston: Harper & Row, Publishers, 1963).

feature of nearly every denomination amongst the churches of this continent is the division—not to say rivalry and, sometimes, bitterness—between those who confine their religious pursuits and allegiances to the personal sphere and those who insist upon the public orientation of authentic Christianity.

The latter can claim an impressive heritage, and today they may also make use of the findings and wisdom of those who ask concretely about the future of Christianity in North America. A recent study by the sociologist-theologians Wade Clark Roof and William McKinney,[9] drawing upon insights of Martin E. Marty, Robert Bellah and others, concludes that the so-called "mainline" Protestant churches must rediscover their *public* responsibility if they are to survive in the pluralistic society and make the kind of contribution for which their doctrinal and historical pasts equip them.

The activistic minorities in all these denominations (and they are, I think, minorities) who seek to serve God in the world by addressing the great public issues and instabilities of our times often manifest an enormous impatience with the ecclesiastical majority, who look to their faith and to the church for personal meaning and succor. The latter, in turn, harbor an often silent but sometimes very vocal resentment of those who (as they are wont to put it) "mix religion and politics." But to persons who have sacrificed their private energies and the healing of their private ills to the greater public good, personalistic religion that renounces political involvement constitutes not only a (highly political!) endorsement of the status quo but is a veritable denial of the Christ, who long before Karl Marx wanted to "change the world." I confess that my own sympathies are with this protest against religious privatism. In so many ways, popular religion on this continent, whether conservative or liberal, seems little more than an indulgence of the pleasure principle. Even when it is accompanied by acts of personal charity and concern for others, it often does not rise above the individualism for which North America is famous the world over.

And yet the life of the individual *is* significant for this faith-tradition. We have witnessed in these times the breakdown of a system of meaning which did not acknowledge that significance and so elevated the collectivity, in theory, that it became oppressive even to the human beings who were its chief ideologues and organizers.

Surely the trouble lies in the fact that these two orientations towards the life of faith easily polarize into mutually exclusive ethical programs, both of

---

[9] *American Mainline Religion: Its Changing Shape and Future* (New Brunswick and London: Rutgers University Press, 1987), esp. chap. 7, pp. 229-251.

which are impoverished because they have become precisely that—programs. They have lost the revelational, christological center of faith and therefore they tend to devolve into ideologies and must be considered idolatrous even when, compared with still less responsible patterns of contemporary human behavior, they achieve much that is morally good.

Religious individualism must from the biblical point of view be named an idolatry of the self; and, with many other Christians, I take this to contain an implicit criticism of unchecked capitalism as well as of the more "spiritualistic" versions of self-improvement. But collectivism, while it avoids the sin of individual egotism, falls into other, equally oppressive forms of existential distortion—including the reduction of the self to a state of dependency and moral stupor, as we are seeing in the revelations that follow upon the breakup of eastern Europe.

These two idolatries, the modern failure of one of which has been plainly demonstrated, the other (our own preferred form) whose failure is still hidden beneath the shell of rampant consumerism, must be named in the churches, and must be distinguished from Christian discipleship. And the theological-ethical criterion on whose basis such a distinction can and must be made is perfectly visible in this ancient prayer—as, of course, it is visible in many other places of scripture and tradition, for instance in the Pauline metaphor of the body and its many members—and its Head!

That criterion is implied, first, in the two words that constitute the salutation of the prayer: "Our Father . . ." Not *my* but *our* Father.[10] The first person plural, which is maintained throughout the prayer, silently militates against individualism and spiritual egoism. Luther notes this in a remark from the *Table Talk*:

> The Lord's prayer binds the people together, and knits them one to another, so that one prays *for* another, and together *with* one another; and it is so strong and powerful that it drives away even the fear of death.[11]

Like the Pauline metaphor of "the body," the "our" and "us" of the Lord's Prayer assume the corporate character of the disciple community, an

---

[10] See the "Sermon on the Lord's Prayer" by Ivo of Chartres (1040-1115) in *Early Medieval Theology*, trans. and ed. G. E. McCracken, The Library of Christian Classics, vol. 9 (Philadelphia: Westminster Press, 1957), pp. 319-320: "The prayer is brotherly; it does not say, 'My Father,' as if praying only for oneself, but 'Our Father,' embracing, you see, in a single prayer all who recognize themselves as brothers in Christ."

[11] *The Table Talk of Martin Luther*, ed. T. S. Kepler (New York and Cleveland: World Publishing Co., 1952), p. 209.

eschatological oneness which, as Luther says, even in the act of praying this community is in process of realizing.

Moreover, this "our" is surely more inclusive than the *koinōnia*; for, like ancient Israel, the Christian community of the covenant understands itself to be a *representative* community; and more particularly is this "priestly" character of its identity associated with the office of prayer. Thus Karl Barth goes beyond the Luther quotation when he insists that the *Vater unser* has a *universal* reference:

> We pray "Our Father" in the communion of this assembly, of this congregation which we call the church (if we take this expression in its original meaning of ecclesia, the congregation).
>
> But even while we are in the communion of the saints, in the ecclesia of those who are brought together by Jesus Christ, we are also in communion with those who do not yet pray, perhaps, but for whom Jesus Christ prays, since he prays for humankind as a whole. It is the object of this intercession, and we ourselves enter into this communion with the whole of humanity. When Christians pray, they are, so to speak, the substitutes for all those who do not pray; and in this sense they are in communion with them in the same manner as Jesus Christ has entered into solidarity with sinners, with a lost human race.[12]

The *public* aspect of prayer is thus not only an unavoidable linguistic feature of this "exemplary" prayer, but it is also christologically reinforced. As the prayer of the Christ, when we make it our own we are brought into solidarity with all for whom Jesus Christ lived, died, and intercedes "at God's right hand"—which (as we must surely insist today) means not only all human beings but all *creatures*. It would be hard to find a prayer more open than this to the whole universe, less fixated on private religion.

Yet this same prayer moves naturally and without a break from the first three petitions, which are clearly public and even cosmic in their thrust, to the last three which are—not (in the usual sense) purely private, but (certainly!) personal: "give us this day our daily bread, forgive us our trespasses, lead us not into temptation but deliver us from evil." The broad, public and (yes!) political dimension of the first group of petitions is joined with the requests for personal wholeness, both of body and spirit, and there is no embarrassment, no suggestion of dichotomy, no "in the second place"; they are part of the same act of humble access. And this is because that upon

[12] *Prayer*, p. 44.

which they depend and to which they give expression is not a system, an ideology, or even a "theology *of*" but a living Presence who, like a father or a mother, understands perfectly well that we are not divisible into public and private "aspects" but have, both as individuals and as *koinonia*, a life that is, simultaneously, internally and externally oriented, and one whose personal and public dimensions intersect at every point. As was said to me by a wise and caring woman who has committed herself concretely to the care of a dozen or so older women: "If I follow one of my old friends around for twenty-four hours, I encounter every one of the great public instabilities of our society." The Lord's Prayer understands and honors that kind of integrity.

III. Realism and Hope in the Lord's Prayer

My third and final observation also arises out of contextual reflection and as an aspect of the interdependence of theology and ethics: it concerns the fearless realism and the equally daring historical hope of this paradigm of prayer in the mode of the tradition of Jerusalem.

A prominent, if not *the* prominent feature of what Ernst Käsemann named "bourgeois transcendence" is its determination to think positively about existence. Every religious institution in North America today is under pressure to conform to this optimistic *a priori*. The more bleak the tone of world events, the more conspicuous societal disarray, the more insidiously are powerful socio-psychic forces at work in the religious community to counter such negations through the ministrations of positive religion.

In stark contrast, the theology of the *Pater noster*—not surprisingly for those who have real familiarity with the Judaic tradition out of which it arises—presupposes and imposes upon its thoughtful users an unrelenting orientation to truth; and the truth that it would have us "turn towards" is truth that is indeed full of promise for life, but as is usual with biblical faith the life that it promises can only be glimpsed by those who are prepared to walk through the valley of the shadow of death.

To begin with, as all but the most inauthentic prayer must needs do, it assumes our utter insufficiency—that is, the insufficiency of the praying ones. That Pharisee of Jesus' contrast with a humble publican used prayer as the occasion for self-congratulation (Lk. 18:10-11); and this false employment of prayer is not unknown amongst us! But true prayer implies the posture of the beggar. *Wir sind Bettler—dass ist Wahr!*—Luther's last written words. In prayer we become honest about our beggarly state; and in this prayer it is plain that our beggarliness is all-inclusive, applying, as we have seen, not only to our personal but also our public needs.

Not only are we beggars in Schleiermacher's sense, ultimately dependent, contingent; we are beggars in Kierkegaard's sense, that is, we are *sinners*. Our need is not only for divine assistance but for radical transformation. And this assumption of our need for forgiveness and renewal of the most rudimentary nature applies as much after fifty years of praying "Our Father which art in heaven" as it does after one. Characteristically, Luther already in 1521 gave expression to his *simul justus et peccator* in the following reference to the *Pater noster*:

> The Lord's Prayer alone is enough to prove that all of us are still in sin, for all the saints must . . . confess that they do not yet do the will of God. . . . Nor can it be said that in these petitions the saints pray over their past sins only, and not over the sin that remains and is present. . . . They are the prayers of men who are as yet partly in the kingdom of the devil.[13]

Christian realism begins with the recognition of our own continuing need as *Christians* for radical transformation; and it would, I think, signal a miraculous conversion of the contemporary church at large if when congregations took it upon themselves to repeat this prayer they recognized that fact in their hearts!

But the realism of the Prayer only begins there. It extends, by implication into all aspects of the life of the world. All serious theology begins with the recognition that the world as it is is not as it should be (Juan Luis Segundo). If we are bidden to pray that God's name—that is to say, God's very person and presence—should be hallowed, it is because in the world as it is God's name is *not* hallowed. If we pray that the reign of God should come it is because it has *not* come; the kingdoms of this world have not become the kingdom of our God and of his Christ. If we pray that God's will should be done "on earth as in heaven" it is because God's will is *not* being done on earth, and woe to those who explain every human tragedy, from premature death to international catastrophe, by calling it "the will of God!" If we pray for the daily necessities of life it is because so many of those for whom, representatively, we pray do *not* have access even to the most basic of those necessities; and if we pray for forgiveness, it is because—partly, I suspect,

[13] "An Argument in Defense of All the Articles by Dr. Martin Luther Wrongly Condemned in the Roman Bull" (1521), in *Works of Martin Luther*, Philadelphia Edition (Philadelphia: Muhlenberg Press, 1930), vol. 3, p. 31.

on account of our guilt as those who possess far *more* than life's daily *necessities*!—we do *not* feel forgiven and must ask again and again, seventy times seven! And if we ask to be preserved from temptations and delivered from evil it is because we know ourselves perfectly well to be the playthings of temptations of every conceivable ilk and to be implicated in evil, including systemic evil, to an extent far too devastating for our consciences to contemplate openly apart from the presence of divine compassion.

Whoever thinks that the function of Christian belief is to ensure the undiluted comfort of the soul will shun such a prayer as this if ever they suspect the depths of disturbing truth to which it is designed to introduce the human spirit. I have heard that in certain congregations of the more opulent species of North American "winners" they no longer sing the hymns of Passiontide, these being too "negative." If such congregations were to delve a little into the Lord's Prayer, with its continuing reminders of what is *not right about the world and us within it*, they might well decide to jettison it as well.

Only those who are oriented towards the truth of the world's and their own wrong are permitted, now and then, to glimpse the righting of things. Faith is not doomed to a bleak and unrelieved conception of existence in this world. *Pessimism* has no more place in the disciple community than has programatic optimism. The hope that belongs to the life of faith is able to discern "the City of God" even in the midst of the "tragic empires" of history. That hope does not despair of history, for the Eternal is providentially at work in time; yet an important dimension of Christian hope is God's judgment of even the best of human communities, for they all fall short of the *doxa Theou*. "History moves towards the realization of the Kingdom but yet the judgment of God is upon every new realization."[14]

Just here lies the significance of the doxological ending of the prayer of our Lord. It may not be authentic historically—that is, as part of the original text that we assume had its beginnings in the rabinically-inclined mind of Jesus of Nazareth; but it is entirely appropriate theologically and ethically. "Thine *is* the kingdom, the power, and the glory, for ever and ever." This is the "glimpse," the world and all life seen through the small window of faith, which enables the disciple community to be honest about what is wrong. This is the "already" that permits the church to be utterly realistic about the "not yet." This is the hope that at once challenges our proneness to despair and allows us to give expression to the data of despair without

[14] R. Niebuhr, *The Nature and Destiny of Man: A Christian Interpretation*, vol. 2, *Human Destiny* (New York: Charles Scribner's Sons, 1943), p. 286.

apology, particularly in the community of faith but also—today especially—in our First World societies, which resist and repress all such data.

Because the reality underneath the reality is *God's* reign we do not have to hesitate when we acknowledge—and tremble before—the reigns of tyrants and oppressors (Barmen!). Because the reality underneath the reality is *God's* power, namely power that adopts the way of weakness because it is the power of love, we do not have to bow to the powers that be—powers that must always *seem* powerful even when they are in the last stages of their decline (Augustine's *Civitas Dei*). Because the reality underneath the reality is *God's* glory, glory "hidden beneath its opposite" (Luther), the glory of the the manger and the cross, we are free to name the bogus glories by which nations and peoples are enthralled—the glory of war, the glory of possessions, the glory of the strong and the beautiful, the glory of empire. We are liberated from the sad destiny of those who must conclude that what *appears* to be so really is so. The Christian ethic, if one may use the definite article, is rooted in this ongoing experience of deliverance from the tyranny of the great god, Fact. Faith does not ignore or minimize the significance of the facts of "tragic empires" and warring kingdoms, the rule of dehumanizing economic policies and established social powers, or the superficial glories that vie for our souls. Faith looks all these facts in the face; it is the more realistic about them because it does not accept their *ultimate* reality.

But let us be clear about it: this faith has nothing to do with spiritual heroics. It is not our faith, and it is certainly not our prayers, which alter so fundamentally the facts that rush at us from every honest newscast; it is the grace by which our faith and our prayers themselves are elicited. "*Thine* is the kingdom, the power and the glory."

> *This* [writes Calvin] is a solid and secure basis for our faith; for if our prayers were to be recommended to God by our own merit, who could dare to utter a word in his presence? Now, all miserable, unworthy, and destitute as we are of every recommendation, yet we shall never want an argument or plea for our prayers: our confidence can never forsake us; for our Father can never be deprived of his kingdom, power, and glory.[15]

[15] *Institutes of the Christian Religion*, trans. J. Allen, 7th ed. (Philadelphia: Presbyterian Board of Christian Education, 1936), vol. 2, pp. 164-165.

SELECTED BIBLIOGRAPHY

compiled by STEVEN RICHARD BECHTLER

THE FOLLOWING bibliography is offered as a starting point for those wishing to do further research on the Lord's Prayer in general or on the particular subjects explored in the preceding essays. The materials included range from devotional literature written for laypersons to highly technical works directed to specialists. Important interpreters of the Prayer throughout history are represented, as are many of the participants in today's scholarly debates. Most of the entries have been published within the last forty years, and only works in English are included, although many of these are translations from other languages.

The bibliography is divided into several sections. Under *Old Testament* are listed works dealing with prayer in the Hebrew Bible. The *New Testament* section includes exegetical and theological treatments of the Matthean and Lukan texts of the Prayer, as well as materials focusing primarily on the setting of the Prayer in early Judaism and the life of Jesus. The *History of Interpretation* section is divided into *Primary Sources,* under which is listed a variety of texts composed during the third to nineteenth centuries, and *Secondary Sources,* which include analyses of historical documents by later writers. Works by twentieth-century theologians, both on the Prayer specifically and on issues pertinent to its interpretation (e.g., the use of "Father" for God), fall under the rubric *Theology.* Finally, *Practical Theology* includes materials dealing with prayer and the Lord's Prayer from the perspective of homiletics, psychology, or pastoral theology, as well as items written for study groups or personal devotional use.

These categories are not intended to be precise indicators of the content of the materials, but heuristic devices, helps for getting started in research. Luther's writings, for example, are listed under *History of Interpretation,* but are clearly of great moment for New Testament exegesis, theology, homiletics, and spirituality, among others. Nor does inclusion of a work under *Theology* necessarily mean that it is beyond the ken of the interested layperson or church study group. To provide further assistance to the reader in determining the usefulness of a given item for his or her situation, series titles are listed whenever applicable. Readers searching for additional materials should consult the following:

Carmignac, Jean. *Recherches sur le "Notre Père."* Paris: Éditions Letouzey & Ané, 1969. [See pp. 469-553.]

Dorneich, Monica, ed. *Vaterunser Bibliographie.* Freiburg: Verlag Herder, 1982.

———, ed. *Vaterunser Bibliographie.* Neue Folge. Freiburg: Verlag Herder, 1988.

I would like to express my gratitude to those participants in the 1991 Frederick Neumann Symposium on the Theological Interpretation of Scripture who offered assistance in the compilation of this bibliography.

Old Testament

Anderson, Bernhard W. *Out of the Depths: The Psalms Speak for Us Today.* Rev. ed. Philadelphia: Westminster Press, 1983.

Balentine, Samuel E. *Prayer in the Hebrew Bible: The Drama of Divine-Human Dialogue.* Overtures to Biblical Theology. Minneapolis: Fortress Press, 1993.

Blank, Sheldon H. "Some Observations Concerning Biblical Prayer." *Hebrew Union College Annual* 32 (1961): 75-90.

Bonhoeffer, Dietrich. *Psalms: The Prayer Book of the Bible.* Translated by James H. Burtness. Minneapolis: Augsburg Publishing House, 1970.

Boyce, Richard Nelson. *The Cry to God in the Old Testament.* Society of Biblical Literature Dissertation Series, no. 103. Atlanta: Scholars Press, 1988.

Brueggemann, Walter. *Israel's Praise: Doxology against Idolatry and Ideology.* Philadelphia: Fortress Press, 1988.

———. *The Message of the Psalms: A Theological Commentary.* Minneapolis: Augsburg Publishing House, 1984.

Greenberg, Moshe. *Biblical Prose Prayer as a Window to the Popular Religion of Ancient Israel.* Berkeley: University of California Press, 1983.

Miller, Patrick D., Jr. *Interpreting the Psalms.* Philadelphia: Fortress Press, 1986.

Westermann, Claus. *Praise and Lament in the Psalms.* Translated by Keith R. Crim and Richard N. Soulen. Atlanta: John Knox Press, 1981.

Bandstra, Andrew J. "The Lord's Prayer and Textual Criticism: A Response." *Calvin Theological Journal* 17 (1982): 88-97.

―――. "The Original Form of the Lord's Prayer." *Calvin Theological Journal* 16 (1981): 15-37.

Barr, James. "'Abbā Isn't 'Daddy.'" *The Journal of Theological Studies,* n.s., 39 (1988): 28-47.

Betz, Hans Dieter. "A Jewish-Christian Cultic *Didache* in Matt. 6:1-18: Reflections and Questions on the Problem of the Historical Jesus." In *Essays on the Sermon on the Mount,* translated by L. L. Welborn, pp. 55-69. Philadelphia: Fortress Press, 1985.

Black, Matthew. "The Doxology to the *Pater Noster* with a Note on Matthew 6.13B." In *A Tribute to Geza Vermes: Essays on Jewish and Christian Literature and History,* edited by Philip R. Davies and Richard T. White, pp. 327-338. Journal for the Study of the Old Testament Supplement Series, no. 100. Sheffield: JSOT Press, 1990.

Brooke, George J. "The Lord's Prayer Interpreted through John and Paul." *The Downside Review* 98 (1980): 298-311.

Brown, Raymond E. "The Pater Noster as an Eschatological Prayer." *Theological Studies* 22 (1961): 175-208. Reprint. *New Testament Essays,* pp. 275-320. Garden City: Doubleday & Co., Image Books, 1968.

Carmignac, Jean. "Hebrew Translations of the Lord's Prayer: An Historical Survey." In *Biblical and Near Eastern Studies: Essays in Honor of William Sanford LaSor,* edited by Gary A. Tuttle, pp. 18-79. Grand Rapids: Wm. B. Eerdmans Publishing Co., 1978.

Davies, W. D. *The Setting of the Sermon on the Mount.* Cambridge: Cambridge University Press, 1964. Reprint. Brown Judaic Studies, no. 186. Atlanta: Scholars Press, 1989.

Davies, W. D., and Dale C. Allison, Jr. *A Critical and Exegetical Commentary on the Gospel According to Saint Matthew.* Vol. 1, *Introduction and Commentary on Matthew I-VII.* The International Critical Commentary. Edinburgh: T. & T. Clark, 1988.

de Moor, Johannes C. "The Reconstruction of the Aramaic Original of the Lord's Prayer." In *Structural Analysis of Biblical and Canaanite Poetry,* edited by Willem van der Meer and Johannes C. de Moor, pp. 397-422. Journal for the Study of the Old Testament Supplement Series, no. 74. Sheffield: JSOT Press, 1988.

Dunn, James D. G. "Prayer." In *Dictionary of Jesus and the Gospels,* edited by Joel B. Green and Scot McKnight, pp. 617-625. Downers Grove: InterVarsity Press, 1992.

Finkel, Asher. "The Prayer of Jesus in Matthew." In *Standing before God: Studies on Prayer in Scriptures and in Tradition with Essays,* edited by Asher Finkel and Lawrence Frizzell, pp. 131-170. New York: KTAV Publishing House, 1981.

Fitzmyer, Joseph A. *The Gospel According to Luke (X-XXIV): Introduction, Translation, and Notes.* The Anchor Bible, vol. 28A. Garden City: Doubleday & Co., 1985.

Gerhardsson, Birger. "The Matthean Version of the Lord's Prayer (Matt 6:9b-13): Some Observations." In *The New Testament Age: Essays in Honor of Bo Reicke,* edited by William C. Weinrich, vol. 1, pp. 207-220. Macon: Mercer University Press, 1984.

Goulder, M. D. "The Composition of the Lord's Prayer." *Journal of Theological Studies,* n.s., 14 (1963): 32-45.

Hamerton-Kelly, Robert. *God the Father: Theology and Patriarchy in the Teaching of Jesus.* Overtures to Biblical Theology. Philadelphia: Fortress Press, 1979.

Harner, Philip B. *Understanding the Lord's Prayer.* Philadelphia: Fortress Press, 1975.

Heinemann, Joseph. *Prayer in the Talmud: Forms and Patterns.* Studia Judaica, vol. 9. Berlin: Walter de Gruyter, 1977.

Hemer, Colin. "ἐπιούσιος." *Journal for the Study of the New Testament* 22 (1984): 81-94.

Hill, David. "'Our Daily Bread' (Matt. 6.11) in the History of Exegesis." *Irish Biblical Studies* 5 (1983): 2-10.

Houlden, J. L. "Lord's Prayer." In *The Anchor Bible Dictionary,* edited by David Noel Freedman, vol. 4, pp. 356-362. New York: Doubleday, 1992.

Hultgren, Arland J. "The Bread Petition of the Lord's Prayer." In *Christ and His Communities: Essays in Honor of Reginald H. Fuller,* edited by Arland J. Hultgren and Barbara Hall, pp. 41-54. Anglican Theological Review Supplementary Series, no. 11. Cincinnati: Forward Movement Publications, 1990.

Jeremias, Joachim. *The Lord's Prayer.* Translated by John Reumann. Facet Books Biblical Series, no. 8. Philadelphia: Fortress Press, 1964.

————. *The Prayers of Jesus.* Translated by John Bowden, Christoph Burchard, and John Reumann. Philadelphia: Fortress Press, 1967.

Lambrecht, Jan. *The Sermon on the Mount: Proclamation and Exhortation.*

Good News Studies, vol. 14. Wilmington: Michael Glazier, 1985. [See pp. 122-150, 169-175.]

Leaney, Robert, "The Lucan Text of the Lord's Prayer." *Novum Testamentum* 1 (1956): 103-111.

Luz, Ulrich. *Matthew 1-7: A Commentary.* Translated by Wilhelm C. Linss. Minneapolis: Augsburg, 1989.

Manson, T. W. "The Lord's Prayer." *Bulletin of the John Rylands Library* 38 (1955-1956): 99-113, 436-448.

Marshall, I. Howard. *The Gospel of Luke: A Commentary on the Greek Text.* The New International Greek Testament Commentary. Grand Rapids: Wm. B. Eerdmans Publishing Co., 1978.

Metzger, Bruce M. "How Many Times Does 'Epiousios' Occur outside the Lord's Prayer?" *The Expository Times* 69 (1957-1958): 52-54.

Moule, C. F. D. "'. . .As we forgive. . .': A Note on the Distinction between Deserts and Capacity in the Understanding of Forgiveness." In *Donum Gentilicium: New Testament Studies in Honour of David Daube*, edited by E. Bammel, C. K. Barrett, and W. D. Davies, pp. 68-77. Oxford: Clarendon Press, 1978. Reprint. In *Essays in New Testament Interpretation*, pp. 278-286. Cambridge: Cambridge University Press, 1982.

————. "An Unsolved Problem in the Temptation-Clause in the Lord's Prayer." *The Reformed Theological Review* 33 (1974): 65-75.

Nolland, John. *Luke 9:21-18:34.* Word Biblical Commentary, vol. 35B. Dallas: Word Books, 1993.

Petuchowski, Jakob J., and Michael Brocke, eds. *The Lord's Prayer and Jewish Liturgy.* New York: Seabury Press, 1978.

Standaert, Benoît. "Crying 'Abba' and Saying 'Our Father': An Intertextual Approach to the Dominical Prayer." In *Intertextuality in Biblical Writings: Essays in Honor of Bas Van Iersel*, edited by S. Draisma, pp. 141-158. Kampen: J. H. Kok, 1989.

Stendahl, Krister. "Prayer and Forgiveness." *Svensk exegetisk årsbok* 22-23 (1957-1958): 75-86.

Strecker, Georg. *The Sermon on the Mount: An Exegetical Commentary.* Translated by O. C. Dean, Jr. Nashville: Abingdon Press, 1988. [See pp. 105-128.]

Tausig, Hal. "The Lord's Prayer." *Forum* 4, no. 4 (1988): 25-41.

Tiede, David L. "The Kingdom Prayer." In *A Primer on Prayer,* edited by Paul R. Sponheim, pp. 107-120. Philadelphia: Fortress Press, 1988.

van Bruggen, Jacob. "The Lord's Prayer and Textual Criticism." *Calvin Theological Journal* 17 (1982): 78-87.

van Tilborg, Sjef. "A Form-Criticism of the Lord's Prayer." *Novum Testamentum* 14 (1972): 94-105.

─────. *The Sermon on the Mount as an Ideological Intervention: A Reconstruction of Meaning.* Assen/Maastricht: Van Gorcum, 1986. [See pp. 90-123.]

Walker, William O., Jr. "The Lord's Prayer in Matthew and in John." *New Testament Studies* 28 (1982): 237-256.

Willis, Geoffrey G. "Lead Us Not into Temptation." *The Downside Review* 93 (1975): 281-288.

Zeller, Dieter. "God as Father in the Proclamation and in the Prayer of Jesus." In *Standing before God: Studies on Prayer in Scriptures and in Tradition with Essays,* edited by Asher Finkel and Lawrence Frizzell, pp. 117-129. New York: KTAV Publishing House, 1981.

HISTORY OF INTERPRETATION

A. Primary Sources

Aquinas, Thomas. *Commentary on the Our Father.* In *The Three Greatest Prayers: Commentaries on the Our Father, the Hail Mary and the Apostles' Creed,* translated by Laurence Shapcote, pp. 1-29. Westminster: Newman Press, 1956.

Augustine. *Commentary on the Lord's Sermon on the Mount.*

In *St. Augustine: The Lord's Sermon on the Mount,* translated by John J. Jepson. Ancient Christian Writers, no. 5. New York: Newman Press, 1948. [See bk. 2, chaps. 4-11, pp. 103-127.]

In *Saint Augustine: Commentary on the Lord's Sermon on the Mount with Seventeen Related Sermons,* translated by Denis J. Kavanagh, pp. 17-199. The Fathers of the Church, vol. 11. New York: Fathers of the Church, 1951. [See bk. 2, chaps. 4-11, pp. 122-148.]

In *Saint Augustine: Sermon on the Mount; Harmony of the Gospels; Homilies on the Gospels,* translated by William Findlay, R. G. MacMullen, and S. D. F. Salmond, edited by M. B. Riddle and D. S. Schaff, pp. 1-63. A Select Library of the Nicene and Post-Nicene Fathers of the Christian Church, vol. 6. Grand Rapids: Wm. B. Eerdmans Publishing Co., 1956. [See bk. 2, chaps. 4-11, pp. 39-47.]

─────. Sermon 56: "On the Lord's Prayer." In *Saint Augustine: Commentary on the Lord's Sermon on the Mount with Seventeen Related Sermons,* translated by Denis J. Kavanagh, pp. 239-257. The Fathers of the Church, vol. 11. New York: Fathers of the Church, 1951.

————. Sermons 56-59: "On the Lord's Prayer." In *Saint Augustine: Sermon on the Mount; Harmony of the Gospels; Homilies on the Gospels,* translated by William Findlay, R. G. MacMullen, and S. D. F. Salmond, edited by M. B. Riddle and D. S. Schaff, pp. 274-289. A Select Library of the Nicene and Post-Nicene Fathers of the Christian Church, vol. 6. Grand Rapids: Wm. B. Eerdmans Publishing Co., 1956.

Calvin, John. *The Catechism of the Church of Geneva.* In *Calvin: Theological Treatises,* translated by J. K. S. Reid, pp. 83-139. The Library of Christian Classics, vol. 22. Philadelphia: Westminster Press, 1954. [See pp. 119-129.]

————. *Commentary on a Harmony of the Evangelists, Matthew, Mark, and Luke.* Translated by William Pringle. 3 vols. Grand Rapids: Wm. B. Eerdmans Publishing Co., 1949. [See vol. 1, pp. 311-329.]

————. *A Harmony of the Gospels Matthew, Mark and Luke.* Translated by A. W. Morrison. 3 cols. Grand Rapids: Wm. B. Eerdmans Publishing Co., 1972. [See vol. 1, pp. 204-213.]

————. *Institutes of the Christian Religion* (1536 edition). Translated by Ford Lewis Battles. Rev. ed. Grand Rapids: Wm. B. Eerdmans Publishing Co., 1986. [See chap. 3.]

————. *Institutes of the Christian Religion* (1559 edition). Translated by Ford Lewis Battles. Edited by John T. NcNeill. 2 vols. The Library of Christian Classics, vols. 20-21. Philadelphia: Westminster Press, 1960. [See bk. 3, sec. 20, pars. 34-49, in vol. 2.]

Chrysostom, John. "Homily 19." In *Saint Chrysostom: Homilies on the Gospel of Saint Matthew,* translated by George Prevost, rev. M. B. Riddle, pp. 130-140. A Select Library of the Nicene and Post-Nicene Fathers of the Christian Church, vol. 10. Grand Rapids: Wm. B. Eerdmans Publishing Co., 1956. Reprint. *The Preaching of Chrysostom: Homilies on the Sermon on the Mount,* edited by Jaroslav Pelikan, pp. 130-152. Philadelphia: Fortress Press, 1967.

Cyprian. *On the Lord's Prayer.*

In *Fathers of the Third Century: Hippolytus, Cyprian, Caius, Novatian; Appendix,* translated by J. H. Macmahon, S. D. F. Salmond, and Robert Ernest Wallis, pp. 447-457. The Ante-Nicene Fathers, vol. 5. Grand Rapids: Wm. B. Eerdmans Publishing Co., 1951.

In *Saint Cyprian: Treatises,* translated and edited by Roy J. Deferrari, pp. 127-159. The Fathers of the Church, vol. 36. New York: Fathers of the Church, 1958.

Cyril of Jerusalem. "Mystagogical Catechesis 5."

In *S. Cyril of Jerusalem; S. Gregory of Nazianzen,* translated by Charles

Gordon Browne, Edwin Hamilton Gifford, and James Edward Swallow, pp. 153-157. A Select Library of Nicene and Post-Nicene Fathers of the Christian Church, 2d ser., vol. 7. Grand Rapids: Wm. B. Eerdmans Publishing Co., 1955.

In *The Works of Saint Cyril of Jerusalem,* vol. 2, translated by Leo P. McCauley and Anthony A. Stephenson, pp. 191-203. The Fathers of the Church, vol. 64. Washington: Catholic University of America Press, 1970.

In *St. Cyril of Jerusalem's Lectures on the Christian Sacraments: The Procatechesis and the Five Mystagogical Catecheses,* translated by R. W. Church, edited by F. L. Cross, pp. 71-80. Crestwood: St. Vladimir's Seminary Press, 1986.

Erasmus, Desiderius. *A Devout Treatise upon the Pater Noster.* Translated by Margaret More Roper. In *Erasmus of Rotterdam: A Quincentennial Symposium,* edited by Richard L. DeMolen, pp. 93-124. New York: Twayne Publishers, 1971.

Gregory of Nyssa. *The Lord's Prayer.* In *The Lord's Prayer; The Beatitudes,* translated by Hilda C. Graef, pp. 21-84. Ancient Christian Writers, no. 18. New York: Newman Press; London: Longmans, Green & Co., 1954.

Ivo of Chartres. "Sermon on the Lord's Prayer." In *Early Medieval Theology,* translated and edited by George E. McCracken with Allen Cabaniss, pp. 317-323. The Library of Christian Classics, vol. 9. Philadelphia: Westminster Press, 1957.

Latimer, Hugh. "First Sermon on the Lord's Prayer." In *Selected Sermons of Hugh Latimer,* edited by Allan G. Chester, pp. 158-174. Folger Documents of Tudor and Stuart Civilization. Charlottesville: University Press of Virginia, 1968.

Luther, Martin. *An Exposition of the Lord's Prayer for Simple Laymen.* In *Devotional Writings I,* translated by Martin H. Bertram, edited by Martin O. Dietrich, pp. 19-81. Vol. 42 of *Luther's Works,* edited by Jaroslav Pelikan and Helmut T. Lehmann. Philadelphia: Fortress Press, 1969.

————. *The Large Catechism.* Translated by Robert H. Fischer. In *The Book of Concord: The Confessions of the Evangelical Lutheran Church,* edited by Theodore G. Tappert, pp. 357-461. Philadelphia: Fortress Press, 1959. [See pp. 420-461.] Reprint. *The Large Catechism.* Philadelphia: Fortress Press, 1959. [See pp. 64-80.]

————. "On Prayer and the First Three Petitions of the Lord's Prayer" and "The Fourth, Fifth, Sixth and Seventh Petitions." In *Sermons I,* translated and edited by John W. Doberstein, pp. 169-182. Vol. 51 of *Luther's Works,* edited by Jaroslav Pelikan and Helmut T. Lehmann. Philadelphia: Fortress Press, 1959. Reprint. *Martin Luther: Selections from His Writings,* edited by John Dillenberger, pp. 215-228. New York: Doubleday, Anchor Books, 1962.

————. *The Small Catechism.* In *The Book of Concord: The Confessions of the Evangelical Lutheran Church,* translated and edited by Theodore G. Tappert, pp. 337-356. Philadelphia: Fortress Press, 1959. [See pp. 346-348.]

Origen. *On Prayer.*

In *Alexandrian Christianity,* translated by John Ernest Leonard Oulton and Henry Chadwick, pp. 238-329. The Library of Christian Classics, vol. 2. Philadelphia: Westminster Press, 1954. [See chaps. 18-30, pp. 274-322.]

In *Origen's Treatise on Prayer: Translation and Notes with an Account of the Practice and Doctrine of Prayer from New Testament Times to Origen,* by Eric George Jay, pp. 79-223. London: S.P.C.K., 1954. [See chaps. 18-30, pp. 136-209.]

In *Prayer; Exhortation to Martyrdom,* translated by John J. O'Meara, pp. 15-140. Ancient Christian Writers, no. 19. New York: Newman Press, 1954. [See chaps. 18-30, pp. 65-129.]

Teresa of Avila. *The Way of Perfection.*

Translated and edited by E. Allison Peers. New York: Doubleday, Image Books, 1964. [See chaps. 27-42.]

In *The Collected Works of St. Teresa of Avila,* translated by Kieran Kavanaugh and Otilio Rodriguez, vol. 2. Washington: Institute of Carmelite Studies, 1980. [See chaps. 27-42.]

Tertullian. *On Prayer.*

In *Latin Christianity: Its Founder, Tertullian,* translated by Peter Holmes, Alexander Roberts, S. Thelwall, and Robert Ernest Wallis, pp. 681-691. The Ante-Nicene Fathers, vol. 3. Grand Rapids: Wm. B. Eerdmans Publishing Co., 1951.

In *Tertullian's Tract on the Prayer: The Latin Text with Critical Notes, an English Translation, an Introduction, and Explanatory Observations,* by Ernest Evans, pp. 1-41. London: S. P. C. K., 1953.

Theodore of Mopsuestia. *Commentary on the Lord's Prayer.* In *Commentary of Theodore of Mopsuestia on the Lord's Prayer and on the Sacraments of Baptism and the Eucharist,* translated and edited by A. Mingana, pp. 1-16. Woodbrooke Studies, vol. 6. Cambridge: W. Heffer & Sons, 1933.

Valdés, Juan de. "Dialogue on Christian Doctrine." In *Spiritual and Ana-baptist Writers,* edited by George Huntston Williams and Angel M.

Mergal, pp. 321-329. The Library of Christian Classics, vol. 25. Philadelphia: Westminster Press, 1957.

Wesley, John. Sermon 26: "Upon Our Lord's Sermon on the Mount: Discourse the Sixth."

In *The Works of John Wesley,* vol. 5, pp. 327-343. London: Wesleyan Conference Office, 1872. Reprint. Grand Rapids: Zondervan Publishing House, n.d.

In *Sermons I: 1-33,* edited by Albert C. Outler, pp. 572-591. Vol. 1 of *The Works of John Wesley,* edited by Frank Baker. Nashville: Abingdon Press, 1984. Reprint. In *John Wesley's Sermons: An Anthology,* edited by Albert C. Outler and Richard P. Heitzenrater, pp. 223-238. Nashville: Abingdon Press, 1991.

B. Secondary Sources

Bahr, Gordon J. "The Use of the Lord's Prayer in the Primitive Church." *Journal of Biblical Literature* 84 (1965): 153-159.

Chase, Frederic Henry. *The Lord's Prayer in the Early Church.* Texts and Studies, vol. 1, no. 3. Cambridge: Cambridge University Press, 1891. Reprint. Neudeln/Liechtenstein: Kraus Reprint, 1967.

Glasson, T. F. "Who Wrote Our English Lord's Prayer?" *Theology* 77 (1974): 252-255.

Jungmann, Joseph A. *The Mass of the Roman Rite: Its Origins and Development.* Translated by Francis A. Brunner. 2 vols. New York: Benziger Bros., 1951-55. [See vol. 2, pp. 277-293.]

Lampe, Geoffrey W. " 'Our Father' in the Fathers." In *Christian Spirituality: Essays in Honour of Gordon Rupp,* edited by Peter Brooks, pp. 9-31. London: SCM Press, 1975.

Rordorf, Willy. "The Lord's Prayer in the Light of Its Liturgical Use in the Early Church." *Studia Liturgica* 14 (1980/1981): 1-19.

Simpson, Robert L. *The Interpretation of Prayer in the Early Church.* The Library of History and Doctrine. Philadelphia: Westminster Press, 1965.

Vokes, F. E. "The Lord's Prayer in the First Three Centuries." In *Studia Patristica Vol. X: Papers Presented to the Fifth International Conference on Patristic Studies Held in Oxford 1967, Part I,* edited by F. L. Cross, pp. 253-260. Texte und Untersuchungen zur Geschichte der altchristlichen Literatur, vol. 107. Berlin: Akademie-Verlag, 1970.

Theology

Ayo, Nicholas. *The Lord's Prayer: A Survey Theological and Literary.* Notre Dame: University of Notre Dame Press, 1992.

Boff, Leonardo. *The Lord's Prayer: The Prayer of Integral Liberation.* Translated by Theodore Morrow. Melbourne: Dove Communications; Maryknoll: Orbis Books, 1983.

Barth, Karl. *Church Dogmatics.* Vol. 4, pt. 4 (lecture fragments), *The Christian Life.* Translated by Geoffrey W. Bromiley. Grand Rapids: Wm. B. Eerdmans Publishing Co., 1981. [See secs. 76-78, pp. 49-271.]

————. *Prayer.* Translated by Sarah F. Terrien. Edited by Don E. Saliers. 2d ed. Philadelphia: Westminster Press, 1985.

Bonhoeffer, Dietrich. "Thy Kingdom Come: The Prayer of the Church for God's Kingdom on Earth." In *Preface to Bonhoeffer: The Man and Two of His Shorter Writings,* by John D. Godsey, pp. 27-47. Philadelphia: Fortress Press, 1965.

Crosby, Michael H. *Thy Will Be Done: Praying the Our Father as Subversive Activity.* Maryknoll: Orbis Books, 1977.

Domeris, William R. "Jesus, Prayer, and the Kingdom of God." In *When Prayer Makes News,* edited by Allan A. Boesak and Charles Villa-Vicencio, pp. 113-124. Philadelphia: Westminster Press, 1986.

Duck, Ruth C. *Gender and the Name of God: The Trinitarian Baptismal Formula.* New York: Pilgrim Press, 1991.

Jai Singh, Herbert. *The Lord's Prayer.* Indian Christian Thought Series, no. 8. Delhi: I.S.P.C.K., 1985.

Kay, James F. "In Whose Name? Feminism and the Trinitarian Baptismal Formula." *Theology Today* 49 (1992-1993): 524-533.

Kimel, Alvin F., Jr. "The God Who Likes His Name: Holy Trinity, Feminism, and the Language of Faith." *Interpretation* 45 (1991): 147-158.

LeFevre, Perry. *Understandings of Prayer.* Philadelphia: Westminster Press, 1981.

Lochman, Jan Milič. *The Lord's Prayer.* Translated by Geoffrey W. Bromiley. Grand Rapids: Wm. B. Eerdmans Publishing Co., 1990.

Lohmeyer, Ernst. *"Our Father": An Introduction to the Lord's Prayer.* Translated by John Bowden. New York: Harper & Row, 1965.

Metz, Johannes-Baptist, and Edward Schillebeeckx, eds. *God as Father?* Concilium, vol. 143. Edinburgh: T. & T. Clark; New York: Seabury Press, 1981.

Schürmann, Heinz. *Praying with Christ: The "Our Father" for Today.* Translated by William Michael Ducey and Alphonse Simon. New York: Herder & Herder, 1964.

Shriver, Donald W. *The Lord's Prayer: A Way of Life*. Atlanta: John Knox Press, 1983.

Thistlewaite, Susan Brooks. "On the Trinity." *Interpretation* 45 (1991): 159-171.

Willis, David. *Daring Prayer*. Atlanta: John Knox Press, 1977.

Practical Theology

Andrews, C. F. *Christ and Prayer*. London: SCM Press, 1937.

Armquist, Irving J., and Louis R. Flessner. "Preaching on the Lord's Prayer (Matthew 6:1-8)." *Word and World* (1990): 81-85.

Ashton, John. "Our Father." *The Way* 18 (1978): 83-91.

Barclay, William. *The Beatitudes and the Lord's Prayer for Everyman*. New York: Harper & Row, 1963-1964.

Capps, Donald. "The Psychology of Petitionary Prayer." *Theology Today* 39 (1982-1983): 130-141.

Carmignac, Jean. "The Wealth of the Lord's Prayer." *The Way* 18 (1978): 137-146.

Clements, Ronald E. *In Spirit and in Truth: Insights from Biblical Prayers*. Atlanta: John Knox Press, 1985.

Dillon, Richard J. "On the Christian Obedience of Prayer (Matthew 6:5-13)." *Worship* 59 (1985): 413-426.

Ebeling, Gerhard. *On Prayer: Nine Sermons*. Translated by James W. Leitch. The Preacher's Paperback Library. Philadelphia: Fortress Press, 1966. Reprint. *On Prayer: The Lord's Prayer in Today's World*. Philadelphia: Fortress Press, 1966.

Hall, Douglas J. *When You Pray: Thinking Your Way into God's World*. Valley Forge: Judson Press, 1987.

Harner, Philip B. "Matthew 6:5-15: An Expository Article." *Interpretation* 41 (1987): 173-178.

Heiler, Friedrich. *Prayer: A Study in the History and Psychology of Religion*. Translated and edited by Samuel McComb with J. Edgar Park. New York: Oxford University Press, 1932.

LaVerdiere, Eugene. *When We Pray: Meditation on the Lord's Prayer*. Notre Dame: Ave Maria Press, 1983.

Lüthi, Walter. *The Lord's Prayer: An Exposition*. Translated by Kurt Schoenenberger. Richmond: John Knox Press, 1961.

Mangan, Céline. *Can We Still Call God "Father"? A Woman Looks at the*

Lord's Prayer Today. Ways of Prayer, vol. 12. Wilmington: Michael Glazier, 1984.

Peters, Jan. "The Many Forms of the One Prayer." In *Prayer and Community,* edited by Herman Schmidt, pp. 26-36. Concilium, vol. 52. New York: Herder & Herder, 1970.

Smillie, B. G. *Blessed Unrest: Prayers for Daily Living.* Winnipeg: Ronald P. Frye & Co., 1985.

Stendahl, Krister. "Your Kingdom Come: Notes for Bible Study." In *Your Kingdom Come: Mission Perspectives,* pp. 72-82. Geneva: World Council of Churches, 1980. Reprint. "Your Kingdom Come." *Cross Currents* 32 (1982): 257-266.

Thielicke, Helmut. *Our Heavenly Father: Sermons on the Lord's Prayer.* Translated by John W. Doberstein. New York: Harper & Row, 1960. Reprint. *The Prayer That Spans the World: Sermons on the Lord's Prayer.* London: J. Clarke, 1965.

Underhill, Evelyn. *Abba: Meditations Based on the Lord's Prayer.* London: Longmans, Green & Co., 1940. Abridgement. *Abba,* by Evelyn Underhill, extracts compiled by Roger L. Roberts. Treasures from the Spiritual Classics. Wilton: Morehouse-Barlow Co., 1981.

Wilson-Kastner, Patricia. *Imagery for Preaching.* Fortress Resources for Preaching. Minneapolis: Fortress Press, 1989.

Wimberly, Edward P. *Prayer in Pastoral Counseling: Suffering, Healing, and Discernment.* Louisville: Westminster/John Knox Press, 1990.

Winn, Albert Curry. *A Christian Primer: The Prayer, the Creed, the Commandments.* Louisville: Westminster/John Knox Press, 1990. [See pp. 17-81.]

Wyon, Olive. *Prayer.* London: Collins, Fontana Books, 1962.